A LION
IN THE
SNOW

ESSAYS ON A FATHER'S JOURNEY HOME

JAMES M. CHESBRO

woodhall press

NORWALK, CT

Lion illustration © TIP TOP/Shutterstock.com

Cover design: Sheryl Kober
Layout artist: Casey Shain
Copyeditor: Tracy Salcedo
Proofreader: Elizabeth Winkler

Library of Congress Cataloging-in-Publication Data available
ISBN (paperback) 978-0-9975437-8-0
ISBN (e-book) 978-0-9975437-9-7

woodhall press

Woodhall Press, 81 Old Saugatuck Road, Norwalk, CT 06855
Woodhallpress.com

Distributed by INGRAM

For Lynne, James, Mary, and Clare

CONTENTS

PREFACE

This morning, when I woke before my three children to write, I imagined seeing my former neighbor, Sam, who lived across the street from our old house, where I wrote most of these essays. We've moved since then, and now live across the street from woods. For some reason my eyes wanted to find him leaning against a tree, smoking a cigarette. I was debating whether to begin something new or to work on an essay-in-progress about my father, which I had started at our old house, where between sentences, my eyes often rested on Sam washing the school bus he drove, edging his lawn, or standing under his portico wearing black slippers, gray sweatpants, and an undershirt, exhaling smoke.

If I wanted to ruminate from a fresh perspective, I thought, why not bring Sam onto the page? How much differently must my life have looked when he peered out his windows into mine. We were different races, different generations, and came from different parts of the country. I sought brief periods of solitude to write when my babies and toddler slept while Sam, a retired man in his seventies, was alone most of the day. His wife arrived home each night from work at seven o'clock and neither of his sons were alive to visit him.

This book isn't about Sam, but he helps me begin populating the landscape of reflection for you. The memories I really want to tell you about are of the places along the path of fathering that won't leave me alone—the places where images of my deceased father flash in my mind with invitations of healing, hope and, ultimately, moments of self-discovery.

First, let me tell you a bit more about Sam. He invited me into his home once. He stopped me in the street, under the motionless oak tree branches in front of his house, like he had done many times, except I could tell something was wrong by the hurried way he spoke:

"You know any carpenters? Do you have a handyman I could call?"

"I don't really have one, no." I said. "Why? What's up?"

Sam turned and waved me in the direction of his front door.

"Let me show you," he said.

I wiped my feet on the welcome mat and gazed up the stairs that bisected the two main rooms. The smell of cigarette smoke lingered in the rugs, couches, and cloth-covered chairs. The wood floorboards creaked under our footfalls through the small dining room, where stacked mail and newspapers sat on a table next to two empty candleholders.

"Here's where they tried to get in, when I was driving the bus," he said when we reached the kitchen. "Busted right through the doorjamb." We both stood there, staring at the cracked wood and the broken glass at our feet.

"I gotta get this secured by tonight," he said. He turned to look at me and added, "And it's already getting late."

A carpenter eventually arrived to fix Sam's backdoor. As I watched him remove lumber from his truck in the dark, I thought about how being in Sam's home unsettled me for reasons beyond the obvious threat to our safety.

Between shifts, during the pleasant months, he groomed his lawn and the hedges. He watered and snipped flowers. He washed his school bus. He wiped each window with glass cleaner. He smoked on his stoop.

Meanwhile, I wrote on the couch in our living room, or at the dining room table, or, before our second child came, in the empty bedroom upstairs, and always with a full view of Sam's white colonial with black shutters. While writing about my father, who died when I was twenty-four, sometimes, between sentences, I wondered how old Sam's two sons had been when they passed away, both of them dying on the Fourth of July in separate years. Sam's life invited me to consider my own from new vantage points, though I don't think I thought about that too much when I lived across from him. He heard the shouts and cries of our children carrying out our windows, while his children were framed in the silent pictures on his wall.

In our neighborhood, one man set off Fourth of July fireworks that rivaled those presented by the city. Parked cars packed our block as families filled the sidewalks, walking to the show carrying lawn chairs. When my son was twenty-two months old, he sat on my knee, looking out his bedroom window, his eyes finding the exploding colors above the rooftops. I saw Sam across the street, standing in front of his house, his head turned toward the flashes in the night. For some, of course, holidays are an occasion of grief, rather than celebration. I wonder now how Sam and his wife, Beverly, could endure such a painful anniversary—the inescapable booming.

Remembering Sam floods me with humility I didn't expect

to experience when memories of him began circling in my mind. We installed child locks on every cabinet, drawer, and door handle. Plastic outlet covers protected curious fingers from electricity. Gates barricaded the crawling, stumbling, diaper-wearing young ones from tumbling down the stairs. And yet, Sam couldn't protect his sons from dying. The day I entered Sam's home, I didn't want to be there because I had stepped into his childless fatherhood.

Eventually, all our children leave us. They go to college. They move out. I want to be present during the highlights we attempt to capture with our cell phones, but also for the incidents when our children push us beyond our human limitations. In writing these essays, I've found the maddening moments to be occasions for new understandings about our children and us. In these essays I've held a match to the wicks of episodes that seemed like universal launching points. What I want to tell you about are the scenes that continue to replay in my mind, the scenes that, like these recollections of Sam, have become invitations and offerings. I've found some truths in the midst of the inescapable booming that explodes inside this son and father.

Let me tell you what I've been invited to see.

Rumbles & Roars

Understanding my father was as unsustainable a
state of mind as euphoria or patience. Maybe I
understood him for a few minutes at a time, and
maybe, for a few minutes at a time, I understood him
better than anyone else understood him, but if I said
my understanding was definitive, I'd be saying that
the man was static, a done deal, a wrapped package,
never slipping out of character or spilling over with
contradictions, never driven by affinities and fears
that even he himself couldn't fathom. By delving into
the riddle of him, I hoped to know his mystery by
finer degrees. Through language could I inhabit him
as much as he had inhabited me. Through language I
could dream that dream called Father.

—BERNARD COOPER

Green Mazes

—ɷ—

In the garage, away from the noises and needs of everyone in the house, I anticipated quiet, but instead the gasoline fumes and the cooing mourning dove made me think of my father. When Dad finished mowing the lawn, I always admired the lines he'd drawn, the way he created a maze of diminishing rectangles. As a boy, from the third-floor window, my eyes traced the outside edge where the wheels of the mower had bent the blades down, the scent of cut grass drifting through the screen. I followed the lines as they ran the length of the yard next to the fence, around the metal swing set in the back, under the pine and oak trees, and then back toward the house. A row of hedges bordered one side of the yard, and I imagined him standing on his wooden ladder trimming them, bending at the waist and leaning forward, waving the electric clippers like a wand.

Green Mazes

The first time he let me push the old red mower I was ten. He spent weekdays and several nights in front of students, so he must have given me some instruction, if only to blurt out, "Follow the lines you make, and don't run over your foot." Maybe Dad watched me from the kitchen window, or from behind the screen door.

It was my turn to make rectangles in the yard while the engine rumbled over the tufts of crabgrass and bare patches. The mower chopped up twigs and needles from the pine in the back, where moss grew over soft black dirt. I bet when I asked him if I could mow the lawn, one corner of his mouth turned up—a look he gave me when we slap boxed. His fingers jabbed into the flesh of my cheeks enough to turn my face, or tapped the top of my head. "C'mon," he said, circling me. "Put your hands up in front of your face. Protect yourself." He always found an opening, and of course, my arms weren't long enough to reach him.

When I finished walking in squares, I called for him, and he met me in the middle of the yard. He pointed to patches of grass. "You missed, there, there, and there," he said. And then he walked back into the house. Maybe he and Mom were arguing that morning. Maybe the weight of being the son-in-law to a millionaire car-dealership owner was too heavy for him, an artist and a teacher.

These are the memories of him that come back when I have a quiet moment to myself. These memories surface because his death has become an extension of the reconciliations we never made. When he died, we were both bachelors teaching high school. We had started to become friends. It was the part of our story that I most wanted to live. I was twenty-four, and he was sixty. The half smirk on his face that said, "You don't know shit yet, kid," had disappeared in our conversations when we ate together. His voice softened when we talked on the phone at night.

Usually I mowed vertical stripes, which make the yard appear larger from the house. But because Dad was on my mind, and it was faster, I began to mow rectangles. The small yard was twelve paces long—boxed in by the side of a detached garage, a row of arborvitaes in the back, a fence, and a deck. After the first several rectangles, I had to stop, tilt the front wheels up, turn, pace, and repeat. I turned and turned and turned, mowing the middle patches of grass, pivoting around in my mind, searching for my father.

I was in my yard as a man, but memory placed me in the middle of the green maze of my childhood, on the day when I first mowed a lawn. He had disappeared behind the thwack of the closed screen door. Squirrels chased each other around a tree trunk. Their claws scratched bark. The mourning dove bellowed its song through the small opening of its beak, in low undulating coos. Branches rustled and wavered in the breeze. Their shadows shifted on the soft spikes. What kind of father am I becoming, and what do the memories of my dad have to teach me as flashes of his figure walk over the lines we've drawn? All around me grass blades bent toward light, and everywhere was green and growing.

Trains

—ᴍ—

Our trips to the city were powered by a current of danger, of our vulnerability to the electricity that throbbed invisibly in the tracks, of the need to walk in haste to avoid strange men yelling at you. Walking behind my father in Philadelphia was like sitting in a train car during those moments when you go underground before the lights come on. He carried me on his heels for a ride through streets I didn't know. I watched his torso shift and his arms swing in front of me. He was my father, and I followed him.

Wherever my father brought me in the city was a secondary excitement compared to the journey there. While we waited on the platform, Dad checked his watch and talked about the voltage on the tracks below. He intended to frighten me away from the painted yellow edge, and it worked. I grew up in my mother's hometown, five miles from Camden, my father's home city. While riding on the Speedline, we watched Camden County whiz by in square backyards. Victorian homes and well-kept properties gave way to the faded black tar rooftops of row homes, abandoned buildings, sidewalks, and parked car after parked car. Our shoulders bumped and our spines adjusted to the jostling passenger car. When we went underground in Camden, the inside lights came on. The Delaware River moved in a swift current below us as we outpaced cars on the Benjamin Franklin Bridge. We went underground again. "Eighth and Walnut next stop. Next stop Eighth and Walnut," said the conductor.

The urgency with which my father walked to nowhere in particular only added to the drama of leaving my safe little town. When I say he walked fast, I mean that for me to keep up, every ten feet or so I'd break into a trot for a few strides. We went to Reading Terminal to eat. We went to the expo center for the boat and car shows. We walked around the Gallery. Each time we passed the Florsheim men's shoe store, he reminded me that he worked there. Perhaps he was proud to be a working member of the city he loved. What did he want me to think about when he pointed out the store?

I think my father viewed each trip as an adventure in teaching me how to conduct myself outside the borders of my sheltered life. Walking fast was one of his ways of overdramatizing potential danger. One bright day in Center City stands out. I was looking at the back of my father's khaki pant legs when a man started yelling at him.

"Hey, you know what time it is?" I looked over my shoulder to identify the person whose voice bellowed at us.

"C'mon," my father said. "Keep walking."

The man's voice was deep and desperate. The words overlapped in a gargled slur. The man shouted again, his voice rising over afternoon traffic braking and honking at the intersection.

"Hey! The time. What time's it?"

We walked toward a group of people waiting to cross the street. A red light flashed *Don't Walk*. The man asked again. My father yelled "four-thirty" over his shoulder and turned the corner.

"That's their trick," my father said. "They get you to stop. Look at your watch. And that's when they do what they want to you."

After my father died, I hated Christmas. When I married, five years later, I told myself to buck up and find some joy in going to a tree farm, and then standing the evergreen in a corner of the living room of the home I shared with Lynne. But I couldn't bring myself to celebrate. Bing Crosby's voice filled in our silence, "offering a simple prayer for kids one to ninety-two." Lynne hooked ornaments on the branches. She adjusted the golden ribbon on the tree, stepped back, and returned to the ladder.

"How does it look?" she asked. Her delight was audible. Each letter of the word *look* rose in pitch.

"Looks good," I said, in a flat tone. *Looks good* contained one more syllable than the apathetic *fine*, or the *sure* I've learned to avoid. In the short time we've been married, Lynne has correctly decoded *fine* and *sure* as pleasantries that mean one of two things: a) I'm indifferent to a matter she cares about, or b) I don't like something but would rather not admit it. The problem with these responses, which may be why they continue to slip out, is that I think I'm being amicable by using them. But they jar Lynne. It might feel like I'm dismissing her attempt to hear my opinion or involve me in making a decision. "Looks good" actually worked when we were newlyweds. She decorated, and left me out of it. My project? Building a monument to my deceased father with his half-century-old trains on the mantel. Merry Christmas.

I placed the old black engine, four cars, and a caboose on the white wood. They were stationed on two sections of metal tracks. A railroad crossing sign, red metal bench, two white signs, and a hand truck filled the gaps around the garland and pine cones above the empty fireplace. The white lights highlighted the dull, nicked metal of the train. Prongs of tarnished steel pointed through green pine on either end of the mantel.

The last time I talked about trains with my father was our last Christmas together. Our plates, stained by blueberry pancakes and egg yolk, lay forgotten in the kitchen sink that morning. We stood in the living room, and I heard the slow drip of the faucet. My sister sat on a red plaid couch, reading a glossy paperback book about photography. Over her shoulder, a stuffed Philadelphia Eagles pennant rested against the beige wall. An astute fan might have traced the kelly green helmet and gray two-bar face mask to the early eighties.

My father stirred his black coffee counterclockwise. The teaspoon clinked around the sides of his cup at a faster pace than the trains. He freed the spoon and drummed the rim three times, then rested it on my grandfather's smoking stand. I don't understand why he kept that wooden-legged tower, since emphysema had killed my grandfather six weeks before I was born. It would make sense only if he associated the smoking stand with his father and not the habit that led to his death. Anytime my father caught a whiff of secondhand pipe smoke, he inhaled deeply and said, "God, that makes me think of my father." Even as a boy, I sensed he was under the influence of something powerful. As he exhaled, he looked away. He was somewhere else, distant and removed.

We both stared at the turning wheels and the oscillating axles. We didn't say much. Glasses framed his vision. He narrowed his eyes. Steam from his coffee rose around his cheeks. I didn't want to disengage the gears of his imagination. He placed his cup on the smoking stand and gave the tired engine a gentle push with his fingertips. He tilted his head so that it was more in line with the wheels and the tracks. We spoke as if we were in church.

"Sometimes you just have to give it a push," he said.

"They still go, don't they?"

"Still go."

"How old are they, Dad?"

"About fifty years old. Engine's just a little tired."

What visions appeared for him on the window seat where his Marx electric steam engine circled the small artificial tree? He had woken up alone on Christmas morning. My sister and I came over a few hours later. He tilted his head to his right shoulder like a boy, like the son he remained, even at sixty years old, standing over a cotton-balled landscape. Maybe the black metal coal cars with *New York Central* written on the side had a delivery for him. Maybe he smelled a pipe.

I fed James his bottle, and burped him in the glider. I bounced him to sleep with his head cradled in my palm, his sleeping face slack and expressionless, pressed against my chest as I paced in front of his crib. During those newborn months, I noticed the red train resting on the white shelf as if it were in a station. I came to think of the toy as a promise, an object of hope for the days when James might sleep through the night. I thought of the toy as a promise of interaction with a newborn who did little more than nurse, soil his diaper, and sleep. The train belongs to a wooden railway collection called Thomas & Friends. Like the others, this train has a name. This train has the same name as my son, my father, and me. I didn't know that the red steam train magnetically coupled to a coal car would pull me back in time. I didn't know that when James held the train in his hand and watched the wheels turn we were departing together, on a journey back to my father.

When James was eighteen months old, I read him *James and the Red Balloon and other Thomas the Tank Engine Stories*. He pointed to the trains, leaned forward, and tapped them on the page as he said their name and color.

Thomas and his wild-eyed friends came to life when we watched the eight- to ten-minute shows on TV. Before bed, James sat on my lap in the La-Z-Boy. He hummed engine sounds. He clapped to the theme song "Hop on Board." He squatted and jumped and jumped and forced me to cover my own tender engine. George Carlin narrates these stories, whose conflict usually derives from a misunderstanding between the train characters. Carlin alters his voice for the dialogue of each train, but a similar crotchety kind of tone you might expect from Carlin puffs from the funnel of each engine. Their eyes move in zany circles to show disbelief, or shift to one side to direct the dialogue to a particular train. The trains release steam. They shunt the disobedient Troublesome Trucks.

I gave James the red train to hold in his hand whenever we stood outside and waved good-bye to his grandmother he calls, Nimi. James yelled, "Bye, Nimi!" but never watched her, staring instead at the rims of her tires. He stared and waved and yelled. And as the rims began to rotate, he increased the pace at which he waved, until he saw Nimi's bumper. James's obsession with the red train brought him to a fascination with movement. When I gave James his red train, he flicked the black wheels with his finger and watched them spin. Then he placed the train on the hardwood floor, rested his head on his arm as he lay down, and moved the train back and forth.

I stood before a wall of Thomas & Friends merchandise at the toy store. I gazed at individual trains, packages of tracks, bridges, windmills, tunnels, and numerous sets. I found a starter set and ignored the advice—Ages Three and Up—stamped on the blue box. The cashier rang up the purchase, which included the grass paper and glue I needed to make James a train table. The cash drawer of the register sprang open, clinking like bells of arrival.

I glued grass paper to plywood and gray pipe insulation to the edges (later on I realized that these were decent ideas, and though aesthetically pleasing, they were ultimately impractical. Green flecks rubbed off onto James's hands and sleeves, and when he was two, he ripped the gray foam border off the table).

When my son first saw the train table I made for him he pushed the red train back and forth with his small meaty hand, lifting it to see the wheels spin, and then returned it to the grooves on the wooden tracks. I never heard of Thomas when I was a boy because he didn't arrive in the States until I was in junior high, which made me wonder how old I was when my dad gave me a set of Lionel trains for Christmas.

While in the attic looking for something else, my eyes often glanced over the big box containing the trains my father gave me, but I didn't ever consider opening the lid I imagined could only connect me to grief. I'd moved my set of Lionel trains from my mother's house in New Jersey to mine in Connecticut, but I couldn't remember the last time I'd actually held them. At the top of the box, next to the red capital letters spelling out *Lionel*, was the slogan: More than a toy—a tradition, since 1900. The black font was easy to read over the picture of faint white mountains. An engine lit the track at the base of a lake, pulling three cars and a green caboose. I lifted up the box to read the small black print on the side: 1983. I was seven.

Boxes of my father's train were stacked next to mine. I wondered how old my father was when he first opened his train set. I tried to picture him near his father's armchair, in Camden, while he read the newspaper, his pipe smoke drifting over them both.

I was looking for a date, but even as I lifted the wax paper and scanned the instructions, manuals, and tracks plans, I knew it didn't really matter *when* he played with his trains. I just wanted these old toys to tell me something about my dead father. Instead, I found the paper used as packing material: a bank envelope, an auto insurance business reply card that said I saved $12.30 on my auto insurance with Allstate, and a Sears, Roebuck and Co. *Catalog Bargain Flash.* Any time I turned one of the catalog pages, fingertip-sized pieces fell to the dusty floorboards.

Dad loved riding trains on the twenty-minute trip into Philadelphia. One Sunday when I was a boy, after Brent Musburger finished taking the CBS audience for a live look around the country's one o'clock National Football Conference games, I asked my father where he was going. He stood on the threshold, his hand on the doorknob. I asked him if we were going to watch the Eagles game together. He smiled and said he had to go to work, closing the door behind him. The glee on his face surely came from the freedom he felt in the city. He worked at Florsheim, a men's shoe store in the Gallery, a shopping mall in Center City. He didn't work at one of the shoe stores at the Cherry Hill Mall, a fifteen-minute drive down the road. Instead, he rode the train and commuted into Philly two nights a week and Saturday morning. During the holiday season, he worked Sundays too.

My father never yucked it up at the country club in town. He didn't play poker, or go to bars. For guy time, my father worked at a shoe store. Once, when I was in college, he told me that during the holidays the manager used to leave sandwiches and beer in the back where they read *Playboy* on their breaks. It was so out of his stern character to divulge such an innocuous secret to me. He was the disciplinarian in our house, the genuflecting Catholic patriarch in the aisle-side seat of our family's pew. He shaved every day and tucked in his shirts.

After returning home from one of his shifts, he held out a pen. It was kelly green with *Eagles* written on the side in gray. "Do you know who gave me this?" he asked. "Ray Ellis. He's the safety. Walked in the store today and bought shoes from me. Big feet," he said. I wonder if it was 1984, the same year I gave him the stuffed pennant. Ellis led the team that season with seven interceptions.

James knows that a purgatory of toys exists in the attic. The floorboards are a wasteland of gifts, some worn out and some unopened. He has developed a keen sense for when the first step creaks. "Oh, Dad. Can I come?" he shouts. On such an occasion, when he was three and a half, even though I thought I had hidden them, James spotted the box of Lionel trains.

He lifted the top off the box and tried to talk, but sputtered, "Dad, Dad, Dad, Dad, Dad . . ."

"OK, James. Why don't we take the engine out," I said.

"Dad, Dad, Dad, Dad," he continued.

I picked him up with one arm and cradled the engine like a football in the other. James kicked his legs and finally spat out, "Dad, Dad, Dad, the box," he said. "Let's bring the whole thing." I placed him on the floor and we looked at each other. All children know when their parents teeter on a balance beam of thought. James could see I stood on one leg, windmilling my arms.

"Well, they're just sitting over there. Aren't they?" I said.

"Yeah, Dad."

I pushed the metal tracks together in an oval on the train table in the living room. Lynne sat on the floor with her legs crossed, next to James. He held the green engine.

"These trains are very special. You have to be careful with them. OK? They were your dad's when he was a boy," Lynne explained. James has seen pictures of my father. And when I told him that my father gave me my trains, I thought it would be the moment when he realized he's never met him. I had almost finished connecting the tracks when I noticed James staring at the engine, fingering the light and the funnel.

We wouldn't be talking about my father's death, though, not that day. I clipped the metal piece to the tracks and plugged in the transformer. The wheels of the Burlington Northern turned, and the train lurched forward and began to career round the small oval.

"Dad, Dad, Dad, Dad!" James shouted. He tried to place his hand on the top of the engine. "Dad, I want to do it." I thought he meant to move the lever, but he wanted to push the train with his hand. I put the transformer away, relieved to have disconnected the electricity from the tracks.

I was sitting at my desk one morning looking at a photograph of my father and me when James walked in to the room. He stared. "Who is that, Dad?" he asked.

My father's arms hung free against a midsection untouched by the sun. He wore a yellow suit entirely too short by modern standards. My nineteen-month-old body stood a foot away holding a red bucket upside down over my head, drops of water splashing circles around me and my shadow, which missed touching my father's feet.

Behind the flesh of his stomach, white water flowed toward us. As my father looked at the camera, his wide grin revealed his upper teeth. His gray hair was unkempt. He stood in the middle of the sheen of water in the lower half of the picture. The Atlantic Ocean extended beyond him in a vast waveless plain.

"That's my dad, James. He's your grandfather the way Papa is your grandfather."

"Where is he?" James asked. I had wondered what I would say when James finally asked this question. Each time the thought arose, I pushed it away as quickly as it came. *Something soft and gentle,* I had thought to myself. *No, you can't bullshit the boy. Be honest. Out with it.* James's brown eyes peered into mine, waiting for an answer. *Heaven. Talk about Heaven.*

"He died."

"Why?"

"He had a bad heart."

"Why?"

"Well, it's kind of complicated, son. He didn't always eat well." I said.

"Maybe he ate nuts," James said as his eyebrows rose.

"Well, not exactly. He wasn't allergic to them. More like fatty stuff. Stuff that isn't good for you. That doesn't make sense, does it?"

"Where is he?"

"He's in Heaven, with God."

"Oh."

"You really would have liked him. Actually, James, you know he had his own set of trains."

"He did?"

"Yes, he did. They're in the attic. Should we go get them?"

"Sure!"

Trains

I brought the black steam engine and coal car to the living room and placed them on the train table. Like my Burlington Northern engine, my father's black steam train was the same 0-27 gauge and fit on James's plastic tracks. He moved the black train back and forth with reluctance, as if he was in trouble.

"What's the matter, James?"

"Dad, I don't want to die."

"I know, James. But it's not something you should worry about. You're so young."

James asked me to couple the black steam train to its coal tender.

"Hey, buddy, do you remember in *Toy Story III* how all the toys were afraid they were going to be stuck in the attic? Well, in a way, you saved these trains. They were stuck up there in their old boxes."

I showed him how to couple up my father's train again and stepped back and watched him discover them. He began narrating the interaction of the trains the way he does with his Thomas & Friends engines, like Carlin on the TV show.

That night after dinner, James was coupling and uncoupling all three generations of trains with the flick of his fingers. He spat out engine sounds through clenched teeth. As I watched my son play, he ignited in me a longing for my father I could not suppress. James struck the red train against the track over and over and over again, like a match to a matchbook. By the time my son went to bed, my mind was aflame with father.

I separated all of my Lionel trains and set them up on the hardwood floor in the living room, in front of the fireplace, below the white mantel. I pushed the steel prongs into the holes of the tracks and made a circle under the tree branches. I plugged the transformer into the outlet and clipped the small metal piece to the bottom of a track. I held the black box in the palm of one hand and turned the steel lever with the other. The transformer hummed then whined as a current surged through the tracks, to the engine wheels, which started to turn. The clickety-clack, clickety-clack rose and fell as the Burlington Northern bustled around the worn steel tracks. The red light on the front of the engine illuminated the wood floor and white molding. I imagined the train racing through the shadows of low-hanging branches on the Christmas morning my father had given them to me, glowing under tree lights. I placed two plastic people on the platform, and waited for a ride.

Footsteps

—〰—

I find my father when I run. Memory needs movement to lead it forward, to give it rhythm and life. After my cardiologist challenged me to make major life changes, I took to the road and listened for my father's encouragement, though as I ran, it often felt as if I was running from his last breaths.

Running became a confrontation with both my own mortality and my father's death. I chose to look at my last moments with him as his final pep talk, a broken plea for me to break the cycle of heart disease. I listened for my father's voice from the sidelines of my boyhood and I listened for him as a man running.

The waiting room of the cardiologist's office was a small convention of elderly people helping each other. They carried canes, ventilators, and each other. Their bodies, as if projecting my inner self, were slow, careful, fragile, feeble, vulnerable, and searching for life. The nurse called their names, waiting in the doorway. They shuffled toward the nurse who rested a clipboard on her hip. She smiled.

Shouldn't I be at happy hour with my friends? I thought. Maybe seeing a cardiologist was an overreaction.

"Twenty-five-year olds don't belong here," I had hoped the doctor might say. "Come back when you hit forty."

Dad survived the heart attack, but two weeks later he couldn't breathe. The cause of death was presumed to be pulmonary failure. I took him to one cardiologist appointment in the time between. Now I've become the patient. Laminated medical posters of hearts and lungs hung on the walls. Every sterile square inch of the office reminded me of sitting next to my father. Perspiration dripped down my sides.

"I'm a little nervous," I admitted to the nurse while I waited for her to give me an EKG.

"Family history?" she asked.

"Yeah. Bet you don't see a lot of people here my age," I said, hoping my youth was an anomaly, hoping for an out, an escape.

"You'd be surprised," she said, raking away patches of chest hair. "I see more and more people in here who are young."

The doctor's voice filled the confined space.

"Tell me something," he said, "Why are you here?" I could tell by the look in his eyes that over the years he has given many people bad news. The doctor sat under one of the two square lights embedded in the drop ceiling. The fluorescent glow produced a reflection in his glasses.

"Because I want to live longer than my dad," I said.

Shortly after my first visit I took a stress test.

"Your EKG looks good," he said. I heard him say the word *normal* in the next sentence and tuned out whatever he said after that. Like a child who hears "Yes you may go out and play," but doesn't hear where he is permitted to go and when he has to return. He suggested I begin taking a baby aspirin.

"Every day?" I asked.

"Every day," he responded. At that point, I wasn't ready to hear any suggestions, so I began admiring his brown Cole Haan slip-ons instead. Subtle white braiding outlined the top of each shoe. The black rubber soles came up a little over the toes, and wrapped around to the heels and a pocket of Nike Air. I've wanted shoes like his for a while. Determining to order a pair was the only decision I was ready to make.

At age thirty-one, with a wife and child, it was time to break through the caution tape I had wrapped around the warning my father left me. My eating habits were irresponsible. I indulged in too much bar food, and started too many mornings with a bacon-egg-and-cheese sandwich. I ate red meat whenever I could. Most Fridays, I ate a bar burger loaded with sautéed onions, crispy bacon, ketchup, mustard, lettuce, and tomato, with a side of fries. My LDL cholesterol had risen to 157. The doctor wanted it under 100.

"Red meat once a week. Bacon once a month if you have to, and thirty minutes of cardiovascular exercise four times a week. And, I really think we should start you on a statin. It's time." He said.

"So I'll take this pill every day for the rest of my life?"

His calm demeanor was disarming. "If you follow these guidelines, you will not have a cardiac event in *my* lifetime."

I didn't want to run. My thighs were heavy, and my feet pounded the pavement in a sloppy, angry trot. Exhaust rose from cars and trucks as they rushed by, and dissipated into the air I breathed. I hocked up phlegm and spat. An eruption of sweat covered my face, stinging my eyes and salting my mouth. After five minutes, I wanted to turn around and walk home. After ten minutes, the muscles in my face relaxed. I picked up my chin and gave in to the soothing rhythm of footsteps and breaths—and my father's voice.

"Keep going," I heard him say, "That's it. You got it." And his voice brought me back to lowering my second baseman's glove toward the loose orange granules of the infield during a Little League game. He stood next to the metal fencing of the dugout and I punched my mitt. He was wearing white sneakers, blue jeans, a navy blue sweatshirt, and the cheap yellow team hat.

As I continued to run, his voice faded, and I breathed harder. I pushed off the street, trying to kick-start Dad's voice again.

Twenty minutes in, after I nodded to the driver who stopped in the intersection, my father startled me again. "Let's go," he said. "C'mon," he said, and I imagined standing on a mat in some loud unfamiliar gym locking up with another wrestler, my father's cheers booming from his cupped hands and igniting a rush of adrenaline. Though I was fatigued, I laughed.

During one such match, my father stood at the edge of the

mat, wearing a red flannel shirt. I had just pinned my opponent in a cradle. I wrestled for most of my youth. My father patted me hard on the head with his open palm. I unsnapped the white plastic chinstrap and walked toward the steps for the picture. I was the lone wrestler on the top step with a blue ribbon, and the only one wearing a cup. When I saw that plastic triangle jutting out of the red spandex wrestling singlet, I realized how absurd I looked. In all the years of practices and tournaments, I never saw anyone else with a cup protruding through their singlet, and apparently my father didn't notice this either because he was adamant that I wear it.

By the time my street came into view, my stomach was sucking in against itself and I was not laughing. I was pushing harder, running faster, gaining ground. "C'mon son," my father said. "C'mon." And I pushed harder. I strode over breaks in the sidewalk. I passed cars stopped at a red light. I ran along the white stripes of the crosswalk. The houses formed blocks. I pumped my arms faster and inhaled greedy, chest-heaving breaths.

I turned up my driveway, walking flop-footed, my hands folded on the top of my head. I stopped and tugged hard on my shorts. The air moving in and out of my diaphragm replaced my father's voice. I had just stepped into my fatherless fatherhood. Sweat stung my eyes and blurred the shapes of old oak trees that lined the far end of the street. The branches hung over slabs of sidewalk and formed a distant tunnel. I tried to picture him then, emerging under the canopy of green, striding toward me through the shadows and above the concrete, but I couldn't see anything.

Sometimes
We Pray Together

—⚏—

I.

All the letters of the alphabet merged into the next on the yellow rubber ball. I don't know why I threw it against the wall next to the glass frame of my mother's wedding bouquet. My parents were yelling upstairs as I fingered the grooves of the dirty letters. Maybe I was testing my accuracy in some risky game I had created, trying to land the ball next to the frame hanging high above my head without hitting it. I think I was nine. The ball squeaked each time the rubber pressed against plaster. Dead petals shook. Perhaps I was trying to shatter the glass and the shouting.

My father stood next to me as dust particles rose above the frame, which was facedown on the floor in front of an aisle of glass shards and crumbled petals. His nostrils flared. The heels of my mother's slides echoed down the hardwood staircase. He jammed his hands against his hips, eyeing the floor, the wall, and the floor again. Without turning his head, my father suggested I go for a bike ride.

I pedaled down Euclid Avenue, past the train station, along Interstate 295, the Jersey Turnpike, across the George Washington Bridge, and through southern Connecticut, until I reached a beige three-bedroom colonial with black shutters. Inside our home, I proposed to Lynne and we conceived a son. Inside our home our son cried, nursed, slept, babbled, and crawled.

One afternoon I spread my arms wide like an airplane. I rumbled engine noises out of my throat to redirect our son's attention, to stop his cries, to distract him from his parents who were learning how to argue. James was our only child then. We thought parenting him was a challenge and it was compared to taking care of ourselves.

My arms reached across the table and over James's head. He tilted his chin up and gazed as I flew over him, which was why I didn't see the ivory-framed sepia photograph of his mother and me dancing at our wedding reception. My wing clipped the frame. It fell from the shelf and crashed to the hardwood floor. His mother laughed, and joked about me being a klutz.

Before I went to the basement for the hot glue gun, I strapped James in his booster seat, above the four ivory pieces, and unbroken glass. I handed him the picture, so he could look at his parents together.

The squabbles my wife and I talked out had more to do with minor misunderstandings than any looming emotional distance that can build between spouses over years. Even TV directors from Bravo couldn't spin our newlywed tiffs into compelling drama. The small pieces of the frame warmed in my palm as I waited for the gun to heat and soften the glue stick in the chamber.

Whenever I notice that frame on the shelf in our home, now, I see the imperfections in the glued frame, and I remember when marriage had yet to humble me.

II.

James cried because he refused to eat his lunch, and Mary started crying because James was crying, but what Mary was really crying about was that she was tired and needed her afternoon nap. Two or more crying people in my house sends me into full-blown fix-it mode. I unlocked the deadbolt and threw open the side door. I brought the stroller out of the SUV and set it upright in the driveway. I walked back into the kitchen and reached for Mary.

"What are you doing?" Lynne asked.

"Taking Mary for a walk," I said. "She'll fall asleep that way—"

"No, she won't. It's way too hot, and even if she does fall asleep, she might not transfer back into her crib," Lynne said as Mary rubbed her face into Lynne's shoulder.

James pulled on Lynne's shirt while crying. "I want the whole hot dog, Mom. The whole hot dog. Not the cut-up hot dog!"

James's hot dog sat on his plate, cut up and cold. It was the last hot dog in the house.

"James, I need you to take a deep breath," Lynne said as she looked down.

"Should I go to the store for more hot dogs?" I asked.

"No," Lynne said.

"Let me try the stroller," I insisted.

"Jamie! That's not helping," Lynne said. Of course, we were both trying to think of a solution, but why the hostile edge to our words? If the dialogue were written with the subtext, it might have gone like this:

Lynne, let me make one of them shut up.

What do you think I'm trying to do here?

Oh, I understand. Since I didn't ask James how he wanted his hot dog, because I cut it up, this is my fault.

As Lynne stared at me, Mary's snot and tears glistened on the shoulder of her mother's shirt. James tried to climb up her leg. "Mommy!" he cried.

If another person touches me right now, I'm going to lose it, is what Lynne's eyes told me.

I opened the side door with my shoulder and forearm, grabbed the handle of the stroller, and stepped like a javelin thrower. I heaved the stroller into the air. It sailed the length of our SUV and bounced off the driveway once before landing motionless on its side. I retreated into the garage and kicked the recycling bin.

I am most incensed when I think I'm trying to help and that my attempt is being rejected, as if I'm trying to make the situation worse. I seethed in the garage, where empty cans and plastic milk jugs settled on the dirty floor. My children cried inside. But this thinking is a detriment to the conflict. It's a spiraling inward, a bruised ego trying to soothe itself.

Part of the soft handle on the stroller rubbed off from the impact of my toss. Sometimes when we take the children for a walk, Lynne notices it and grins at me. And I'll grin back as if to say "I know, that was ridiculous." But my grin hides my embarrassment. And my anger, when Lynne and I argue, hides an undercurrent of anxiety that takes hold of logical thought and pulls it under the surface of my tremendous fear that we'll end up like my parents.

III.

I dismounted my bike and let it fall to the brick sidewalk, the metal kickstand clanged against the bike frame as I ran up the steps of the porch of our first house. I was eleven.

Once inside, I called out. "Whose ugly car is that in front of our house?"

The front door to our duplex opened up to the dining room. Before I could finish my sentence, I saw Mom weeping in a chair. The chair sat apart from the table, next to the entrance to the kitchen and in front of the landing to the stairs, and immediately, I wished I were in any other room. Her legs were crossed. Her elbow rested on the arm of the chair, and she held a tissue. Her eyes remained on the windows for a moment before she fixed them on me.

"Ask your father," she said.

Dad sat in his wingback chair in the living room. His chin rested in the palm of his hand and his pointer finger pressed against his temple.

"Did you buy that car, Dad?"

"You wouldn't understand," he said, waving his hand in my direction as if I were a fly in front of the news he watched on TV. "It's complicated."

"But, Dad it's a Ford. How could you get a Ford?" I asked. Mom's father owned a Buick dealership. I overheard my grandfather and my uncles rank the class of automobiles produced by General Motors, many times, and Cadillac was the best, then Buick, and then the others.

He rose and walked toward the window, looking in the direction of the two-door Ford. It was maroon with a strip of wood paneling. The maroon vinyl reflected the glare of afternoon rays. "I don't know. How could your uncle try to rip me off?"

"He ripped you off, Dad?"

He waved his hand at me again. "I shouldn't have said that." Mom blew her nose in the dining room.

"That's not what happened, Jim." Mom said.

"How would you know, Kathy? You weren't in his office when we were negotiating."

"I could hear plenty from the hallway, while I tried to distract the children from hearing you both curse," she said.

"Oh please, Kathy. What do you know about negotiating a car deal?" And he laughed, perhaps imagining her doing so.

"If you were still working there, maybe I wouldn't have to clip coupons each week and walk around the Acme punching a calculator."

Dad stood and walked into the dining room. His arms were straight, and his fists were clenched at his legs. He stared at

Mom, then me, as if daring me to speak. When neither of us did, he climbed the stairs until he was in his office, in the attic.

IV.

The engine idled. I could see him from the front window of our new house. Over the railing of the wraparound front porch, and down the slope of the front lawn, he rested his chin in his hand. His other hand hung over the wheel, tapping the dash. My father sat in the driver's seat of his car, waiting. My mother was upstairs. How did I know they were going to see a marriage counselor? Surely my father didn't offer up that information. Perhaps I overheard, or perhaps Mom told Katie and me. Maybe she felt like she had to validate leaving us in the house by ourselves. We were old enough, though, both in middle school.

What was I thinking as I watched my father tap the dash while my mother walked around to the passenger-side door? Dad kept looking at his wrist. They were late. The sound of AM news radio spilled out of the car when she opened the door. My heart lifted when I saw her. Her dress flounced as she stepped. Her dark hair kissed her shoulders and her back as it waved when she turned. Seeing a marriage counselor must have been her idea. I can't imagine Dad saying to her, "Listen, I'd really like to talk more about our emotional distance and why our arguments have intensified. Let's talk about our feelings, Kathy. I would really welcome the opportunity to be vulnerable with you and a third party."

Third parties existed in my mind as people who spoke at you when you were in trouble. Like at school: your guidance counselor, the assistant principal, the aide in the classroom, the learning specialist, the tutor. I rooted for Mom's beauty to soften Dad's anger. But I wonder if it only incensed him more. They were late after all and Mom's beauty might have only antagonized his dormant longing for her affection. Perhaps Mom hoped it could awaken a new attention in him, that he might open up to the counselor and to her.

V.

Streetlights glowed in the neighborhoods we whizzed by in her speeding car. Mom went to daily Mass whenever she could. When I became an altar boy, sometimes I served the 6:30 a.m. Masses. Mom drove us in the predawn darkness. She was a nun for a year. She was twenty-one. It might make for a better story if I could say that my father lured her out of her vows and her clerical habit, but she simply wasn't happy.

"You get special graces and blessings for going to Mass," she said as she drove. "And you get even more for being so close during the consecration." I gazed at the priest from my kneeler on the marble altar. I was so close I could hear the priest's robed layers shift around his shoulders and torso as he raised his arms toward the lights shining down from the ceiling. With a wafer in his fingertips, he said, "This is my body, which has been given up for you. Eat it and you shall live forever."

As an altar boy, I believed that my mother believed that the priest believed the wafer he held had really become Jesus. I wanted to believe in the consecration, that what I witnessed was a miracle. I held the wood handle of the gold paten beneath the hands of the people as the priest placed the Eucharist into their palms, to catch any crumbs that may fall. When members of the congregation walked up to the altar and held out their hands, their eyes mirrored the awe I began to feel for the Eucharist. I followed the wafer with my eyes as the priest lifted it with his straightened arm, handing it to their open hands.

I witnessed my classmate, Eddie, pretend to put the Eucharist in his mouth then show it to another kid in the aisle of a pew. He revealed his teeth, a devilish grin, and then turned over his hand with the Eucharist in it. No one likes a tattletale at any age. But in fifth grade, it's a terrible sin. I feared my mother and God more than Eddie, so I coughed up the information in the car ride home, to relieve myself of the burden.

My father drove us home from Mass. Katie and I were in the back seat.

"I think Eddie Monroe didn't eat the Eucharist," I said. My mother turned to look at us.

My father looked in the rearview mirror. Mom grabbed the top of the seat to face us. "What did you say?"

"I think I saw him put it in his pocket," I said.

"Are you sure?" Dad asked.

Eddie was a class clown. I didn't want to cause him trouble, not out of any sense of loyalty, but because I didn't want to become an object of his ridicule.

"Yeah, I'm pretty sure," I said.

Mom turned to look at Dad's profile. "What should we do, Jim?"

"I don't know," Dad said.

"What's the big deal?" Katie asked.

"Some people take the Eucharist home and do sick things to it because they're angry at God," Mom said.

"Like who, Mom?" I asked.

"Creepy, Satanic people," Mom said.

"I'm sure the kid isn't a devil worshiper, Kathy," Dad said.

Mom frowned. "I'm calling Monsignor when we get home," she said.

Monsignor went to Eddie's house and investigated. I had never been to Eddie's house, but I imagined him sitting between his parents on a couch, the Monsignor's Adam's apple moving up and down over the white space of his collar. Monsignor had gray hair, glasses, and a stern upright posture. He didn't say much to us altar boys before or after Mass in the sacristy.

I imagined him interrogating Eddie. "Now you said that you placed it in your pocket then what?" Monsignor called my mother to report that Eddie consumed the Eucharist before he left the church. She didn't have much else to say about the Monsignor's visit to Eddie's house. Luckily for me, Eddie and I just avoided one another at school.

VI.

The girl next door to our second home had blonde bangs, which she moved with her fingers after she smiled at me. Our arms and hands touched when we played jail break, or run the bases with her two siblings and my sister. We all wish we could go back and talk to our younger selves, but man, do I wish I could have a serious sit-down with my adolescent self who looked at all girls as potential wives.

As my hormones raged, my mother came home from a

pilgrimage in the former Yugoslavia, where she reported visions of Mary, the mother of Jesus, had appeared to seven children. Mary gave them messages to share with the world. Two of those messages involved saying the rosary as a family and fasting on bread and water on Wednesdays and Fridays. When Mary appeared, the sun spun and people fainted. After Mom's pilgrimage, she came home from Acme with grocery bags of bread and bagels and rolls. On Wednesdays and Fridays we ate bread and drank water. Sometimes we prayed together.

While in Mom's car, I mentioned a girl from my class. Mom took that as her green light to give me "the talk." Not a biological explanation of reproduction, but instead a religious perspective, which she seemed to think her son should know immediately.

"Kissing is fine. But anything else is a sin," Mom said.

"Mom!" I shouted.

"Yes, any sort of touching is a sin."

"Please stop talking."

"I'm sorry, Jamie, but your body is a temple of the Holy Spirit."

"So, I have to wait for marriage to do anything?" I asked.

"Yes, your body is sacred, Jamie," Mom said.

Maybe I turned up the radio or changed the subject. She used to be a nun. She drove me to Mass in the morning, and told me about sin in the afternoon. It was her way of loving me.

The way I coped with the escalating arguments between my parents, my desire for girls, and my fear of sinning, was to imagine my wife. "When young we think there will come one person who will savor and sustain us always," writes Brian Doyle in his essay "Joyas Volardores." After a predictable spat between my parents settled down and they each gave up for the night, it's how I comforted myself. But now I realize, as Doyle states, ". . . this is the dream of a child, that all hearts finally are bruised and scarred, scored and torn, repaired by time and will, patched by force of character, yet fragile and rickety forevermore, no matter how ferocious the defense and how many bricks you bring to the wall."

As I write, I'm thinking about a commercial for light beer. The one where a guy is crying at the airport because he doesn't want to leave his girlfriend. His friends laugh in the background.

The girlfriend rolls her eyes and says, "But it's only two days." Once seated on the plane, they make fun of him for ordering a light beer without as much taste as the light beer they've ordered. They tell him drinking that brand of light beer is the second unmanly thing he's done that day. When I was in high school, I drank cheap, warm beer, with my friends behind my parents' garage when they started to divorce.

VII.

A boy never wants to see his mother cry. In my juvenile mind, Dad seemed to be the source of Mom's sadness, and her tears undermined him. My father made a cameo on the bluestone showroom floor of my grandfather's Buick dealership, as a car salesman, for one summer. The time was so brief Mom and my oldest uncle, who ran the business, can't think of much when I ask them about it. He worked nights and some weekends, while also employed at the shoe store in Philadelphia. Selling cars part-time, in addition to his salary and benefits as a public school art teacher, seems so obvious a solution to me now. Wouldn't that have been the financial bump to assuage their strain? While I'm curious as to why he didn't like the job, I wonder if more money would have really improved their marriage.

The last year of my father's life was my first as a teacher. We visited each other. We talked on the phone at night. We were bachelors, becoming friends. As we talked, I imagined him in his dark bedroom, holding the phone to his ear. His forearm draped over the covers that he had pulled up to his chest. The moonlight lit up the carpet in front of his bed and cast a shadow of the windowpane on his covers. I told him about cracking my voice in my last period of the day and how my all-male freshman students had erupted with laughter.

"Well, that's not so bad," he said. "One of my first years, I started class and a few kids were laughing and I had no idea why, so I kept talking. I wrote something on the board and when I turned around they laughed even louder. Finally, I stopped, and a girl in the front seat pointed at my groin. I had just gone to the bathroom and the bottom of one side of my shirt was caught in the zipper and it looked like, well, you know."

"What did you do?

"Turned around, rezipped, wrote something else on the board, and kept talking until they settled down."

"Good story, Dad."

"Well, twenty-nine years in the classroom, and that's the stuff I remember."

"How's the bachelor pad?"

"Ah, Jamie, you know, I'm home in the afternoon before I go out again to teach night school. There's nothing on TV then but *Oprah*. It gets lonely as hell here sometimes, but I can come and go as I please. No one to answer to."

I empathized with my father because I didn't have to answer to him. My independence freed us both to interact and engage one another as men. He didn't have to grant me permission for anything, and I didn't have to ask. When we saw each other, we held out our hands and shook. I didn't need to ask for money, or make sense of my parents' arguing. He wasn't an authoritarian; he was simply an authority in the same profession. And sometimes he was lonely. I don't know if God's grace showered down on me through the ceiling of the church as I knelt at the feet of priests who consecrated wafers. But in the year following college graduation, when I spoke to my father, my resentment dissipated in our camaraderie as teachers and bachelors.

VIII.

Over Jim's shoulder, through the dormered window and the bare branches, city lights twinkled with a pulse a little slower than my own. The palms of my hands dampened. Plumes of carbon monoxide billowed over the black body of the Long Island Sound. Jim sat before me with his legs crossed. We bowed our heads, and he said a prayer. Jim was a Jesuit priest to whom my boss, the president of the prep school where I teach, had introduced to me. However ironic, he goes by Jim, the same nickname as my father.

"So," he said, in an even tone that never pitched with fabricated hope, "How are you doing today?"

I talked to Jim for the first time the spring before my father died. I could only pray to Mary, then. I believed in God the Father, and I believed that my dad and I could continue to grow in our newfound friendship. But I feared upsetting God as I feared anything I might say to my dad on the phone when we talked, that I might sound weak or incapable of independence. After my father died in mid-August, I met with Jim a few times a week.

Medical personnel found him slumped over his steering wheel at the entrance of the ER. My father popped two aspirin for the pain in his chest and drove himself to the hospital. I'm unsure if he was dead for seconds or minutes. I imagine the heart monitor whining the alarm of a flatline, the doctor saying, "Clear," placing the defibrillator paddles on his chest. The second time, his heart began beating again. He came home for two weeks. His lungs started bleeding, and he couldn't catch his breath.

I arrived in Jim's office wringing my hands. I bounced one leg. My eyes darted between his glasses and the lights over his shoulder. Eventually, I could sit still between our long pauses, his large body absorbing my nervous energy. I'd spew weepy, incoherent tangents toward him. And he sat there. We'd make another appointment. I returned. And slowly, over the months, in the pain, I found anger. In the loss of my father, I felt I had also lost my heavenly father. My Lord, and my God had abandoned me.

Jim sat up in his chair one night, looked at me through his glasses, and said, "Jamie, have you ever told Him how angry you are?" Yes, the capital *H* Him. "Go ahead," he said with a shrug of his shoulders, while leaning back in his chair, the fingers in both hands splayed and turned up. "He can take it."

Like other university administrative offices, Jim's was in the old mansion. I descended the winding gray sidewalk with the building looming behind me. If "He could take it," then I was going to give it to Him that night. *Let's have it out, Jesus,* I thought. The certainty that campus security had locked the chapel inflated my blasphemous audacity, and the invisible watermelons I carried under my arms. The undergraduates were home during the semester break. The concrete dissected the frosted ground into an *S* shape. A sliver of faded yellow hung in the dark sky, unsure if it wanted to reveal itself through wisps of clouds drifting in strains, unable to connect. Flecks of light from the street lamps speckled the dark shades of purple and blue stained glass. From a few steps away, the windows appeared as rectangular ink stains rounded off at the top. How many times had I grasped the brass handles to the chapel?

Carolyn taught me how to administer the Eucharist. She was an assistant chaplain, and a mother figure to many of the students who knocked on her office door. As a freshman, I sat on the blue carpet in the chapel as she sat on the step below the altar and talked about the symbolic meaning of giving and receiving the Eucharist.

I fingered the beige dots patterned around my feet as she spoke, "We'll talk a lot more about being reverent to the Eucharist, about the importance of showing reverence to the body and blood of Jesus, but I'd like to start by talking about what it means to be reverent to each other," she said.

She held up a blue booklet. About twenty of us students sat on the carpet, leaning on our hands or legs, listening. "You're probably used to seeing these booklets during exams, but I want you to use them to record the times when someone else gave you Eucharist in a figurative way this week. Maybe they gave you some coins for the laundry machine, or notes from a class you missed, whatever. No act is too small. Write it down in here. And when you gave someone else Eucharist, write that down as well."

Perhaps what I liked the most about our meetings were the open talks we had at the end. We sat in a circle, and for the first time I heard my peers wondering, aloud, about God. At the Jesuit school, we studied a minimum of five religion and philosophy courses. The discussions from those classes became part of our meetings. Being a Catholic became more than being good or bad.

After I graduated stained glass replaced the clear panes. But during my undergraduate days, you could see the great green lawn descending to the steps of the library. You could see the blue waters of the Long Island Sound. Light descended upon us in lanes from the windows. It fell on the blue carpet and the heads of those seated around me. If I still had that blue book, I'm sure the entries would seem trivial. But it wasn't so much what I wrote down as it was performing or receiving acts of reverence, and thinking about them throughout the day, which ensured I'd have something to enter between the light blue lines of the paper. During examinations, I wrote in blue books, knowing I would be judged by the rightness or wrongness of my thoughts. Chronicling acts of reverence in blue books conjured up the twin anxiety of writing for the judgment of professors and God.

After graduation, we e-mailed. Carolyn took me out to eat. And in an ironic role reversal, at my father's funeral, I gave her the Eucharist. When she stepped to the altar and opened her hands to me, one on top of the other, out of all the sympathetic eyes that landed on mine that day, Carolyn's shot through the outer shell of unfeeling I resolved to have to walk down the aisle. At the time, I thought my father would have liked me to administer the Eucharist and give the eulogy at his funeral, but fulfilling these roles required that I perform them. Or maybe these roles were my way of pursuing the atonement I desired. Maybe when I saw Carolyn at Mass in the chapel in the months after my father died, I was still performing. Going to Mass became an obligation.

During sophomore year, a handful of friends and I said the rosary together in the chapel. We called them *Regis rosaries*, because that was the name of our dorm. One night during the week, I entered the empty chapel. I carried a statue of the Blessed Mother from the foyer to the altar steps. The wood was light in my arms, and holding her, I lowered my neck and resisted the urge to kiss the grain of her cheek, even though I wanted to awaken the mother in this statue, to be her son. I wished her eyelids would flip open in recognition of my prayers to her.

I placed the two wrought iron candleholders from the altar at Mary's feet for my prayer group. I didn't turn on the other lights in the chapel, so only the two flames glowed on our shyness of praying together.

One of my buddies in the group was a guy with long blond hair. We called him only by his last name, Wallace. Wallace said even his mother called him Wallace. The rosary has five decades, each consisting of one Our Father, ten Hail Marys, and a Glory Be. We took turns leading the prayer for each decade. The leader said the first half of the prayer, and the other three or four people said the rest of the prayer together. Sometimes the leader stumbled over the words. We were nervous. We were praying together. Wallace liked to hold the beads in one hand, and an empty plastic Gatorade bottle in the other. Between Hail Marys he'd spit his tobacco juice in the bottle.

When Wallace forgot the words, he just made them up. "Hail Mary, full of grace, the Lord is with thee. Blessed art thou among holy women, and blessed is the rolling green grass, and the holy flowing vine." We let him carry on until we couldn't help but burst out laughing.

Before my father died, I believed that reverence was the pathway to the divine, or at least the attempt to communicate with the divine. I saw my actions as those of a sinner who needed to earn worthiness of His redemption. Carolyn taught us to bow deeply and slowly when we reached the altar while processing in for Mass as Eucharistic ministers. When the candle is lit above the tabernacle, He is present. Genuflect before placing the consecrated hosts back in the tabernacle. I believed in a show-and-tell God. Be a good altar boy, don't touch girls, show Him your devotion, and then He will listen to your prayers. My father sucked away any anger I had toward him when he gasped for air on the floor of his house where he died. I transferred all my anger onto God the Father. When Jim said "He can take it," I determined to tell the God I feared He had abandoned me. *You failed*, I thought as my heart hammered in my chest. My fists clenched and unclenched as I stepped toward the doors. *That's what I'm going to tell you, when I'm in there. You fucking failed. And now I'm fatherless.*

The brass handle was cold. I prepared for the door to resist my pull, rattling in confirmation. Locked. But it gave. Cold air disturbed the stillness. Small narrow flags waved above me in the foyer. The doors settled behind me. No air moved out of the heating ducts. The lights were off.

On either side of the taller, hand-carved statue of Saint Ignatius holding a staff, Saint Joseph and the Virgin Mary stood guard, just as they had a few years ago, when my small prayer group met.

"He can take it," Jim said.

I stormed around blue cloth seats and thought about hurling them. Didn't He overturn tables in the Temple? I opened and closed my fists. My hands shook. The thought of hearing my own voice terrified me, so I sounded off from within. *Where were you? He died right in front of me. He's fucking gone. Dead. Where were you, Jesus? I was eating Cheerios. Dad said to call 911. He couldn't breathe. I couldn't save him. The EMTs couldn't save him. I watched them carry him through the kitchen and out the open garage door. Where were you?*

My hands opened and closed in the stale, chilly air of the chapel as I remembered the muggy August air that floated into my father's kitchen, and the ticking wall clock. One flame flickered above the tabernacle. The thought occurred to me to turn around. *Turn around!* an internal voice insisted. Brown, deep-set oval eyes stared out from the man's narrow face. His lips were parted. The corners extended outward and did not imply a smile or a frown. His eyebrows pointed up where they almost came together in the middle. A thin, dark beard framed his slender face. Next to the right side of his jaw, his index and middle fingers formed a peace sign on the large banner. I sat down in the last row and stared at the flame.

I thought about being with my father when he died, about being in the house he rented, when his landlord, who was also his cousin, walked in. The EMTs had carried my father out on a stretcher. I picked my head up from the kitchen table of my youth and said, "He's dead."

"Do you need a ride to the hospital?" my father's cousin asked. In the car we sped by a metal chain-link fence covered in green weeds. We drove to the hospital where my father was born, in the city where he grew up. No train tried to race us on the tracks below the fence. I flipped open my phone and deleted my father's number.

Static voices and people in green scrubs scurried in my emergency room memory. My father's cousin said he would be back. The doctor said they tried everything. He thought it was a pulmonary failure. His lungs bled, which is why when the cop walked into Dad's house with oxygen, before the EMTs arrived, my father continued to gasp for air.

I'm not sure why, but the doctor asked me to see my dead father. Maybe it was to identify him, or perhaps to pay my last respects. A Franciscan monk stood in the room with me. Rosary beads hung from the white rope around his waist. I looked up once at my dad. He lay on a bench in the small room. Thin paper covered his body to his neck. The end of a white plastic tube jutted out of his open mouth. His eyes were still open.

I turned around and said to the monk, "Can you please close his eyes."

"Yes," he whispered. "Might he have a ring on or anything you might want?"

"No. He's divorced."

"Some divorced men still wear a ring."

"He doesn't."

He removed Dad's watch. The monk said a prayer. I kissed my father's forehead. My lips pressed against the wrinkles on his still-damp skin, which was pale and cool. The monk's brown robe swung around his stark white legs. He walked me into another room. The sign on the wall next to the doorless opening read QUIET ROOM. A woman in green scrubs and short blonde hair introduced herself and sat down beside me. Fluorescent overhead lights reflected in her glasses. She talked about an autopsy.

My mother walked into the room.

"Jamie!" Mom said.

Perhaps my father's cousin had called her. It was clear from her anxious eyes that she didn't know he had died. At the time I wasn't thinking about how she spent seventeen years as his wife, or that she mothered two of his children. Or that when she saw my face, sometimes she may have been reminded of what my father looked like when he was younger, when she loved him. I didn't appreciate that part of her would need to grieve too. Since their divorce, I saw them as separate people. When my mother shuffled into the Quiet Room, she walked into the realm reserved solely for my father, which had become sacred space in his death.

I'd spent my father's final days caring for him, sleeping in his bed while he slept downstairs in the hospital bed he rented. I began to know the steps in his house that creaked and those that didn't as I stood behind him, watching him rise on his right leg, the left following. He said it was easier to climb the stairs that way. The hospital gave him a teddy bear to hug when he coughed so that the incisions down his chest wouldn't rupture.

His voice roused me out of sleep, calling my name, asking me to help him up to go to the bathroom, or to make him coffee. I wrapped my arms around him to right him, and my fingers pressed into his cotton undershirt. Most of the time, he watched the Eternal Word Television Network and the History Channel in his pajamas.

One afternoon, as Dad watched a monk on TV talk about the afterlife, I asked, "Dad, did anything happen when—I mean, did you see anything?"

"No," Dad said, shaking his head.

My sister had been at our maternal grandparents' shore house. We took turns staying with Dad. Neither of us could stand watching our father so vulnerable and weak, lying there each day on the hospital bed, with one hand on the remote, the other palm turned up, and his toes indifferently flailed outward. Our father didn't look sixty. He looked seventy, seventy-five, and he seemed to be aging by the minute. The thin, gray hairs on his forehead receded farther back, the wisps matted down and sparse. The white and gray stubble on his face did not camouflage his pale skin; the listless blood cells in his veins were growing more and more recalcitrant.

Caring for our father was what we should have done as his adult children. We washed his pajamas and underwear and sheets. Some of my father's cousins, whom I'd met only a few times, dropped off food. One afternoon I made him a tuna-fish sandwich on whole wheat bread, with baby carrots on the side. Dad scrunched his nose when I handed the plate to him. My mother's absence became a presence, in a way. Caring for our father was a reminder to my sister and me that our parents had divorced. Katie was twenty-two, I was twenty-four.

In the Quiet Room the woman in scrubs persisted. She wanted to persuade me to sign a form so they didn't have to do an autopsy. My mother sat beside me and touched my arm, which felt like a wound so fresh it was still opening.

"He's dead, Mom." I said. And she covered her mouth and cried into her hand as the nurse spoke at me.

"It won't bring him back," the woman in scrubs said.

Thin black lines intersected the bright white floor. I scrawled the name I shared with my father on some forms. My father's cousin came back, sat down, and looked out the window.

After letting these flashbacks play as I stared at the flame that flickered above the tabernacle, I rose to leave. My father's lifeless eyes pointed toward the ceiling, the monk closed them. Carolyn opened her hands to me. The kitchen wall clock ticked, and my father's cousin entered. I saw Jim seated in his chair. I walked past them all. The chapel heaved when I opened its door, their faces trailing me like clouds of breath.

IX.

We sat across from each other, fingering the initials others had carved into the table, and opened up like the bottles of beer had in the bartender's hands, our inhibitions falling to the sticky floor with the caps. I had been attracted to Lynne ever since the first time I saw her in the fall of that year. After two rounds of beer and almost a year later, I waited for her to come back from the bathroom.

She walked past me to her seat, tucked her brunette hair behind her ear, and smiled at me. One of my buddies told me to watch her body language. "It doesn't lie," he had said. "That's how you'll know if she's into you." *She has to be interested*, I thought. Otherwise why would she go out with me? There was the minor problem of her boyfriend and their seven-year relationship. If she was really unhappy with him, wouldn't she have dumped him? She had interned as a guidance counselor last year. That spring we were in the same graduate education class together. The buildings where I teach are filled with adolescent boys who often smell like a hamper. When Lynne appeared in the hallway, or my classroom, the beauty of her petite frame, brunette hair, long eyelashes, and full lips was a smack to the face of my senses. She'd walk into my classroom before the bell rang, to give me a message about one of my students, or to ask me about an assignment for our course. As her heels clicked in the empty hallway, I was left staring at a room full of quiet freshmen. The most coherent thought I could expel was to point to the kid in front of me and say, "Peter. Start us off with the Our Father today." And as Peter said the prayer, I leaned on the desk, my heart thumping under my shirt.

"Listen," I said, holding the empty pint glass and sliding it back and forth on the table. "I can't help but wonder what things might be like if you were single?"

"Me too," she said. Her big, light brown eyes smiled. It was the first time I allowed myself to love her. And it was that moment that I first came to know her calm demeanor. Acid churned in my stomach. And as soon as I heard her voice respond, everything in me relaxed. The fermented barley and hops swelled in my head. Someone at the bar burst out laughing above the buzz of conversations around us. The waiter stopped at our table to ask us if we wanted anything.

"I think we're good," I said.

X.

Our guests stood on the parquet dance floor with the bridal party. They clapped and waited for the DJ to introduce us. Lynne held my hand. Candles illuminated wedding pictures of our parents and grandparents on the side table in the foyer that connected the hallway where we stood and the grand entryway to the stairs and dance floor. My father seemed so much bigger to me than my mother, as their image attracted my attention. My parents were the only couple represented on the table whose marriage ended in divorce. To my young and idealistic mind, marriages were both successful and happy, or failures that ended in divorce. This ignorance made me feel ashamed of my parents. My father's black-and-gray hair was parted on the side in the picture.

As the DJ spoke in words that rumbled together, "And now for the first time . . ." My father's sideburns climbed down past his ears. And the form of his face expanded, "let me introduce . . ." The smile lines widened. His head wavered with the flame reflecting on the glass frame.

"Mr. and Mrs. James Chesbro." the DJ said. We walked past the coffee table. My father's face hovered ghostlike above all our guests.

The next morning, I looked out the window of a van on our way to the airport. We passed other cars on the highway, trees, and exit signs. My bride held my hand and her fingers wrapped around mine. She admired our hands and the white gold and diamonds on her ring reflecting light. I remembered seeing my father's face again, in the moment before we were introduced.

"I had to get you a wedding present," Dad's voice erupted inside.

I didn't allow myself to miss him on our wedding day. He had been dead for five years. And when I heard his voice, I tried to gulp back down all of my grief, in a van with Lynne and strangers. On the plane I told her about how I thought I heard my father's voice. I thought about how the vision of his face illuminated and floating above the coffee table was an instant, a flash—about how much I had wanted him to be there, how much I have always wanted to believe his spirit can still speak to mine.

XI.

At first, marriage was easy. All of our stuff was in the same place, and we didn't have to make plans to be together. What to have for dinner was a fun question, a new question. The real stress came when the new glow of the monitor lit up our room. The light flashed when James's infant cries crackled through the speaker. Was he hungry? Did he have gas? Should we let him soothe himself back to sleep? And if he didn't need to nurse was it my turn to wake up with him?

It was during James's newborn months that I reached for my father's wedding band, which I used to keep in my bedside table. When I was alone, I used to bring his thin ring out into the light. I missed him. But I really held the ring because the emotional distance I felt from Lynne stirred up feelings about my parents, about being their son. I pretended to believe that my father's dead skin remained in the letters and numbers of the inscription KJO to JCC 6-22-74, while the nicked rounded outside glowed. My father's gold ring slid with ease over the wrinkles of my knuckle. Yellow gold clinked against my platinum wedding band.

As I fingered my parents' initials, I thought about the time I had to push my mother and father apart, how each of them had kept their hands to their sides. My mother saw our second house as her dream home, and my father didn't want the divorce. He refused to move out, and my mother refused to cook for him. I was whisking an egg in a pan over the gas stovetop to eat for dinner. The more they yelled and the closer they stepped toward the other, the faster I whisked. Their faces were blistered with anger and enflamed with a resolve to confront the other until finally I put my hands up. My father's sternum and my mother's chest bumped each other. "OK, enough." I said. "Enough."

I never saw my mother and father hit each other with anything other than words. Mom made it to the landing of the stairs. Whatever they had promised each other in Christ the King church on 6-22-74, or on the honeymoon, or thereafter, had been broken. Dad watched Mom climb the steps for a moment. I stood in the foyer.

He raised his hand and pointed at her. "Kathy, you go to your room!"

Mom stepped on the landing and spun around. She held the glass tightly in her fingers and launched the cola and ice cubes in the air. The soda splashed on my father's head, dripped down his face and neck and shirt and forearms, and maybe even some of the liquid touched the ring he wore. The cubes landed on the hardwood floor like the first great balls of hail during a storm. Mom made it to the top of the steps and into the room they once shared. Her voice reached us below, but even as she shut the door, I couldn't tell if she was laughing or crying.

Dad shouted to the ceiling. "My lawyer is going to hear about this!"

He looked at the brown pools of soda stretching out around his feet like fingers of rubber gloves that had been pulled. He saw me watching him, and said, "Clean this up."

I used to take out my father's ring when Lynne and I argued. As I held up the ring to the light, I remembered the time Lynne said to me, "Just because we're arguing doesn't mean we're like your parents." Which seems obvious enough, but the arguing reminds me of my parents. And so here is my question: As an adult, at a remove from the experience, what do we do with painful memories when they surface? As an adolescent, the pain grew into an intense anger and resentment toward my parents.

But at some point, that pain must evolve into an attribute. I want to know what purpose it can serve, other than existing as burdensome recollections I'd rather not think about.

I put the ring in a safe deposit box in the bank. Eventually, I didn't need to take it out anymore to remind myself it didn't fit.

XII.

For five years, Lynne and I forgot about the wedding pictures of our parents and grandparents that we displayed at our wedding reception. We left them in a bag in the attic. Lynne wanted to hang these pictures on a wall in our home. I didn't want to look at the wedding picture of my parents. But when James was almost four, and Mary was fourteen months, we decided perhaps we should put up those pictures.

My parents don't embarrass me anymore, and I'm not trying to escape them. There is nothing for me to free myself from but lingering adolescent anger and lies. It was a great lie I told myself that more money or a marriage counselor could fix my parents' marriage. It remains a great lie I tell myself when I fall into the trap of trying to *fix* a situation. A new battery can fix a beeping smoke alarm. Mortar can fix loose brick steps. A new spark plug can fix a puttering lawn mower. In becoming a father, I've learned that upset spouses and children aren't for fixing. In becoming a father, I've learned to wait for the children to stop crying, because they always do. Perhaps a father's greatest tool is patience.

Forgiving our younger selves of ignorance, it seems, is a lifelong act. "I think we are well advised to keep on nodding terms with the people we used to be, whether we find them attractive company or not," writes Joan Didion in her essay "On Keeping a Notebook." "Otherwise they turn up unannounced and surprise us," she continues, "come hammering on the mind's door at 4 a.m. of a bad night and demand to know who deserted them, who betrayed them, who is going to make amends. We forget all too soon the things we thought we could never forget. We forget the loves and the betrayals alike, forget what we whispered and what we screamed, forget who we were."

I suppose I write these scenes down, here, because my younger self demands I remain on nodding terms with him, that I don't ever forget my parent's marriage. What possible function can these painful recollections serve other than to humble me?

Sometimes at night, after the kids are asleep and Lynne has shut off her phone and I've shut off the game on TV, and we've said we're sorry to each other for not having more patience or being more empathetic, sometimes we're both still angry. I lie on my side of the bed and recount my case. I list all the ways I feel misunderstood and my heart starts pounding. But eventually I give up my internal pity party. I know she's still up too. She'll turn on her side away from me. I'll kick the comforter off my foot. Don't go to bed angry, right? Sometimes we pray together. We say an intention out loud for the other person. And it really helps us reconnect. But midweek, when we've hardly made eye contact and we may be thinking about what we want to accomplish tomorrow at work, we don't pray. We don't talk. We're tired. I know we're not my parents. When I see their wedding picture on our wall, I think about how unhappy they must have been. And I'm humbled enough, as my parents' son, to reach for Lynne's hand. Her fingers curl around mine. Our breaths steady, and our chests rise and fall, like those of our children in the other rooms.

Shore Break

—ɯɯ—

In the summer of 1988, on the 87th Street beach, I discovered how to ride the force of a wave standing up on my boogie board. One morning in June, as I trudged out of the ocean, I met Mike, the lifeguard. He climbed down his stand with his backside to the rungs. He was tall with round shoulders. Dark curly hair framed his face. "Hey, you're pretty good," he said, standing in front of me. "You been riding for a longtime?"

"Since I got this." I said, lifting my new Mach 10 Morey Boogie board a little from my waist.

"Try staying back more. That way you won't catch the front edge and nosedive. And I know there aren't as many people over where you were, but try to stay closer to the stand next time you go out. By the way, I'm Mike," he said. He held out his hand for me to slap. I was eleven years old.

While my father worked, Mom, my sister, and I often visited my grandparents at their shore house in Stone Harbor, New Jersey. During the academic year, Dad taught in the art department at Cherry Hill High School West. He spent almost his entire teaching career in room A-10. In summer he worked on the grounds of the school, landscaping the sprawling fields. When he came home it was hard to get between him and the news, since he wheeled the TV stand from the center of the room and positioned the screen directly in front of his chair. My mother's voice, on the other hand, was always there to narrate as I made sense of scenes.

As a working husband with children, I understand Dad's fatigue now. And since my parents' arguments rose as unpredictably as rogue waves, I can understand why Dad wanted to tune everyone out. My grandparents' shore house served as a welcomed cease-fire from the violence of my parents' shouting. Dad usually had to work, and when he did come "down the shore," which is a phrase those in the Delaware Valley use no matter the geographic orientation of their homes in comparison to their vacation destination, he only made occasional visits to the beach. Instead he preferred to sit on my grandparents' dock and read in the shade, or to walk through town. In his absence I latched onto Mike, the way struggling swimmers hung onto him until he could bring them back to shore. I watched beautiful women flirt with him. I watched his girlfriend, Amy, visit him between the shifts of her part-time job in town. Unlike my father, Mike gave me hope that I could grow up to become the kind of guy who was loved by women.

The day I met Mike, Mom asked what the lifeguard wanted

as she smoothed out the sand in front of her chair with the soles of her feet. My grandparents had joined my mom and sister while I was in the water. "He gave me a tip," I said, "and told me to stay closer to the stand."

"Oh that's nice," Mom said. "Do you want a snack? I have Twizzlers, Tootsie Roll pops, and peaches." I asked for Twizzlers and Mom handed them to me. The licorice bloomed out of my hand like the limp red stems of headless flowers.

"Why don't you go see if your new friend wants any," she said.

As I walked to the lifeguard stand with the red licorice, I saw Mike talking to two girls. Their tanned bodies and string bikinis reminded me of the girls in the background of the advertisements for surf companies that I ripped out of magazines and taped to my bedroom walls. They looked at Mike the way the girls looked at the surfers and bodyboarders in the magazines. "This is my friend, Jamie," he said. "He stands on his board."

"Really?" one of the girls said. "How cute, Mike. You have little friends. Well listen, we should go." She walked a few strides, and I was about to hold my candy offering up to Mike when she turned her head over her shoulder and her brunette hair flipped away from her face. "Maybe we'll see you out tonight," she said. She turned her body and her profile accentuated her round breasts and butt.

"Want some?" I asked Mike.

"No thanks, that's real nice of you, though."

He released his arms and swung them back and forth. When his palms pressed together they made a clap we could hear over the murmur of shore break. I could see my grandparents reading. My sister, Katie, dipped her hand in a bucket of wet sand. The white stem of a lollipop danced out of Mom's mouth as she peered up from under the brim of her hat and through her sunglasses to watch me talk to Mike.

Of all the girls that sauntered before Mike, the only one I ever saw him hug was Amy. And she's the only one who ever really talked to me. Amy had short blond hair cut below her ears. The pale skin of her palm touched my lower back as she bent at the knees, her soft voice asking me if I counted how many girls had visited Mike. She asked me about the waves. She asked me if I was going to be a surfer. Amy only had a few moments before returning to her job in town. She never wore a bathing suit, only shorts and a tank top, since she was always visiting the beach during a break or right after her shift had ended.

Mike and Amy's faces disappeared in a haze of sun as she pulled herself close to him and he dipped his head to meet hers. Their lips touched and they muttered good-bye and made plans for later. We watched Amy dig a trail of footprints up the beach.

"Do you like her, Jamie?"

"Yeah."

"I like her a lot," Mike said.

Before I met Mike, my first lessons about riding waves came from *Bodyboarding* magazine. I lay in my bed in the corner of my room and studied every detail from the magazine pages I placed on my wall. The company names were printed in colors matching the riders' bright yellow, green, magenta, and turquoise board shorts, rash guards, and wet suits. Between the pictures I taped stickers of company logos I had bought in the surf shops in Stone Harbor: Rusty, Billabong, O'Neill, T&C Surf Designs, Gotcha, Local Motion, Sex Wax, WRV, Rip Curl. They also gave me outdated posters when I asked for them. I wore flowered print shorts commonly referred to as Jams, the name of the company that made them. Among the splashes of fluorescence that lit up my beige walls and my mind were the frames of bodies I studied, in hopes that the positioning of their hands and feet on the boards might teach me something about how to ride.

Sometimes I knelt on my bed for a closer look at the feet and legs of a bodyboarder who, unlike all the others, stood on his board like a surfer. Most riders glided along the face of waves on their stomachs. Others rested on their back knees with the soles of their front feet gripping the board. I can't remember the name of the man who gave me the idea that I too could stand on my board like a surfer, but the company logo BZ was stamped onto his board and the page of the ad.

With a lean muscular frame and brown skin, Mike looked like one of those guys on my wall. He could teach me how to be like them. Unlike my dad, he could teach me how to surf.

I brought more into my room than wave-riding fantasies. Interspersed with the ocean blue waves and the logos printed in colors of highlighters were the girls in bikinis. I became aware of them at first the way children are nonsexually aware of their parents' bodies at the beach. A mother shows more of her legs, a father his chest. But as I examined the bodyboarders more closely, the women in the upper and lower corners of the ads won my attention. I noticed their breasts and cleavage. The bottom parts of their suits were high-cut triangles and the straps around their waists rose over their hip bones in the high fashion of the '80s. Most of them stared at the men in the picture, but some stared at me, and when I stared back, a new awareness of the opposite sex stirred in my gut and in my Jams. I wanted to ride waves for the sake of riding. But an equation was forming, a naive, oversimplified, and elementary thought that beautiful, curvaceous women go for the guys who can ride waves. And even in my uninhibited imagination, I doubt I ever consciously considered how my equation worked for guys who didn't know how to ride, guys like my father who made cameos on the beach, fully dressed in sneakers, pants, and a tucked-in T-shirt.

I understood the relationship between the wind and the waves no more than I understood Mike and Amy's relationship, my parents' marriage, or my surging awareness of the opposite sex.

The force of waves "comes from the wind transferring its energy into the water over a stretch of miles (a distance technically known as 'fetch')," determines Susan Casey in *The Wave: In Pursuit of the Rogues, Freaks, and Giants of the Ocean*. In the Atlantic Ocean, when I saw swells approaching from the horizon, it appeared like a mass of mountain-shaped water traveling toward me, "but the water in a wave doesn't actually travel with the wave toward shore," says J. B. Zirker in *The Science of Ocean Waves: Ripples, Tsunamis, and Stormy Seas*. Most of the water moves up and down as the energy of a wave propagates toward shore. "When a wave rises in the ocean and appears to race across the surface, that specific patch of water is not really advancing—the wave energy is," explains Casey. "It's like cracking a whip. As energy passes through the ocean, it spins the water molecules in a roughly circular orbit, temporarily lifting them."

I rode waves in and out of the ocean. My parents argued; Mike and Amy kissed, their emotional energy spilling over onto the shore break of where I stood.

Mike gave me one of his red mesh Stone Harbor Beach Patrol lifeguard shirts, which I had to tuck in or else it draped around my knees. I carried his torpedo-shaped flotation device while running with the guards as they exercised.

When we finished jogging, Mom stood between Mike and me. Two guards lifted the lifeboat to the water, the oars banging against the sides of the boat.

"Thanks for being so good to my son," she said.

"Oh, no problem," Mike said. "He's fun to have around."

"I'm Kathy," Mom said, extending her freckled arm.

"Mike."

"I know. Jamie talks about you a lot."

"I heard you had a good time miniature golfing last night," Mike said. "I love miniature golf. I haven't played yet this summer. Hey, you know what? If it's all right with you, Kathy, maybe Amy and I could take Jamie and Katie one night."

"Mom, I don't talk about Mike all the time."

"You do enough that I know who Amy is," Mom said. Then smiling, she told Mike, "Sure. We're here until Tuesday evening."

In the ocean, I slipped down swells, gliding ahead of the white water until the frothy surge caught up to me only to belch me back out again. Sometimes the waves broke again over the sand-bar and I glided all the way to shore. On one wave, I fell in front of the lifeguards' throne. My feet slapped toward the stand, breaking the surface of the thin pools of shallow water. The lifeguards were still laughing when I stood before them, my hand cupped against the sunshine. I asked if any of them had any Sex Wax.

"Sex Wax?" one of them said. "Do you even know what that is?"

"Yes," I said. "I'm all out. My foot just slipped and I need to rub some on my board."

"You don't rub wax on a boogie board, man, that's only for surfboards," one of them said. At the surf shops, in addition to stickers and magazines, I also bought the puck-sized circular packaged wax. The pucks came in different colors, but I can only remember white, and the vanilla scent released by tearing off the plastic wrapper. And what about that name, *Sex Wax*? I expelled the phrase to the guards, but certainly not at the dinner table with my family. The word sex is an embarrassing one to say or hear in front of your parents, of course, but more to the point, the company name belonged to the surfing culture, a culture decidedly separate from my family. Mike lowered himself down from the stand. He rubbed his hand on my board.

"I can see the foam can be slippery. Keep your weight back, right? Otherwise you'll pitch forward, especially on the take-off. I tell you what. Are you going to be here for a while this afternoon?"

"Yeah. Why?"

"Well, I was thinking about surfing today after work. If it's OK with your mom, maybe I could give you a lesson."

"Be right back." I ran to where my family was sitting.

"Mom," I said, huffing in the salt air, "Can Mike give me a surf lesson today after the guards leave?"

"Yes, that would be fine," she said. "We should go back for lunch soon. Get out of the sun for a while, and then we can stay later this afternoon."

As I stood there with my back to the ocean, I saw my father walking past the dune fencing, where the sun baked the soft sand that burned any sucker who thought they could prance through it without flip-flops or sandals. Dad wore his white sneakers, tube socks, khaki pants, and a tucked-in gray T-shirt. The brim of his white baseball hat was pulled so low over his face he had to tilt his chin up to see where he was going. The logo of our football team spread its kelly green wings across his hat.

"Hey, everybody," he said.

"Hi, Dad," Katie and I said.

"Here, Jim. You can take my chair. I was just about to go in the water," Grandma declared. Dad started to say something polite, and Grandma cut him off while she stood and pulled her black rubber bathing cap from her beach bag. "Go ahead," she said. "I need a good swim. Kathy, there's cans of tuna in the cabinet above the sink if you get back before I do." We watched her walk toward the water playing with the strap under her chin.

"Hey, Dad. You came." I said.

"Well, I thought I'd come see you guys before I head back home. I want to beat all the shore traffic, so I'll be leaving soon." he said.

"Dad, Mike the lifeguard is going to teach me how to surf today." I said.

"Is he, really? With one of those fiberglass boards?"

"Yes."

"With the sharp point at the end of them?"

"Yes, Dad. It's totally safe."

"Is it?"

"Do you want to meet him? He's the tall one sitting in the middle of the stand over there." Mike's arm hung over the edge of the bench and behind the guy next to him.

"You know about this, Kathy?" Dad asked. The shore break crashed through the base of the stand and flattened into clear water before disappearing into the dark gray sand.

"Yes, it should be fine, Jim. I've met him a few times. He's nice. And he's certainly big enough to save Jamie if he falls." Dad's eyes landed on mine as we squinted at each other. His chin was tilted up and he studied my face. He resisted the urge to say more. He sat in Grandma's chair and looked at Katie digging with her shovel.

"We were just getting ready to go back for lunch," Mom said. "Do you want a ride back?"

"No, no, no, I like to walk," he said, waving his hands in front of his face as if they could block the glare of the sun. He stood up. "See you guys at the house," he said. My eyes followed him as he pushed through the sand in his sneakers. As he walked, he raised one arm or the other for balance. A whistle blew. A nearby mother called her children's names. Seagulls hovered over my father's head, circling in the wind with their beaks pointed down. I asked Mom why Dad didn't like the beach.

"Well, he said he got sun poisoning once when he was a

boy, so he doesn't like to stay out in the sun."

His white hat dropped below the dune fencing and the grass. "How did he get sun poisoning, Mom?"

"I don't know, Jamie," Mom said as she exhaled. "I guess his mother didn't put sunscreen on him. That's why I make sure you kids have plenty on. You can't stand it when I rub it on your face in the morning, but it's better than getting burned. You both ready for lunch?"

My father never even considered making a scene in front of his in-laws. So, envisioning him pulling me aside and walking along the shore, the white rubber soles of his sneakers releasing themselves from the wet sand, telling me why he didn't want me to surf, something about all the broken arms he'd seen on his students that skateboard, that he didn't want me to get hurt, that the ocean was dangerous—that scene only exists now in my imagination, constructed completely from speculating the sources of his resistance. He never said he didn't want me to ride a surfboard. But in the triangular shape of the conversation with my parents, I sensed the forces of each of them, pulling in separate directions.

When they argued I often wondered why, and I often wondered who was right. Dad didn't forbid me from trying to surf. He didn't make me choose a side, and six years later when they began to divorce he didn't make me choose then either. While I sensed Dad didn't like me riding a surfboard, as a kid I didn't trouble myself with his uneasiness.

At five o'clock, the guards stood on the stand, blew their whistles, and waved everyone out. I met Mike at the shore. Our feet sank in the wet sand. "Have you ever ridden a surfboard before?" he asked.

"No."

"All right. No problem. Are you goofy or regular?"

"What?"

"Which foot do you put first?"

"My right."

"OK, my friend. That means you're goofy-footed." He knelt down and wrapped the Velcro leash around my left ankle. "Let's go," he said, and he carried the board as our legs splashed through water. "Hop on," he said. I lay on the board and traced the large black *R* of the company's logo toward the triangle tip of the board. "Here comes a few breakers," he said. "Grab the rails." I knew from the magazines that surfers plunged the noses of their boards under the white water while paddling out, but Mike just lifted the nose over the charging walls.

"Almost there," he said as his chest and ribs appeared again when he stood on the sandbar. "All right, sit up and put your hands on the rails. Lift your butt up a little and feel the way you can move the board and keep your balance. Good. Let's turn you around with your back to the waves."

Mom watched us from her chair.

"Now, when a good one comes, thrust the end of the board farther in the water," Mike said. "Let the rails slide past your legs, and when you do it you'll feel the board shoot back out of the water. Then lie flat, keep your chest up, your head turned to see the wave, and paddle with all you got."

I noticed Amy striding on shore, in her predictable khaki shorts and dark tank top. When she saw me her arm shot straight up and she waved. Her sandals dangled from the hand resting on her hip. Her free hand tucked her blond hair behind her ear. She waved again when she saw Mike turn his shoulders toward her.

Mike waved back and sighed. "Oh man, I love her, but it's getting kind of serious."

I waved to her, and she waved again, lifting her body up on her toes. I wanted to tell him I loved her, too. He jumped with the swells that rolled through as the circular orbits of energy rotated under the surface. These smaller waves continued to bob me up and down as we waited for one with enough energy for me to ride. We both kept our eyes on Amy, but how did I look at Mike? Even at age eleven, I understood he was too young to be a father, and yet he seemed too old to be a brother. He was like the cool uncle, in the sense that he gave me attention and didn't have to discipline me. Maybe I became part of the picture that Amy imagined too. I had dark hair and admired Mike the way she might have imagined their own son looking up to the tall lifeguard ruling over a family Amy may have wanted. "She's really pretty, Mike," I said.

"She is, isn't she? She's got it bad though, my friend. She's a bit too serious. She's a little older than me. Wants to move in together after I graduate from Tufts. But I'm thinking about grad school on the West Coast."

"So you can surf. Right?"

A smile ripped across his face and he laughed. "Right. Why am I telling you all this, Jamie?" I shrugged my shoulders. "Well, let's keep it between us, OK?" he said. "Wow! Here comes a good one." Before I could turn to see the wave, I felt him lift the tip of the board. "Let the board move between your legs," he said. He pushed the board into the water and it released in front of me, and the burst of the surging board surprised me. "Paddle, paddle, paddle!" Mike shouted. The swell rose under me and soon my paddling no longer contributed to the speed. I did a push-up and planted my feet on the long white surfboard. Before the wave broke, I flipped forward, somersaulting underwater, the leash on my ankle pulling my left leg toward Mike. When I came to the surface, I coughed and spat and wiped away a strand of snot. Amy ran out into the water past her knees. "Are you OK?" she called over the stampeding white water charging beyond her.

"Yeah," I said, and raised my arm in case she couldn't hear.

Mike pushed water away from his torso with cupped hands. "What happened, friend?"

"I think my feet were too far up the board."

He smiled and spread his arms out as if it were the punch line of a joke. "What have I been tellin' ya all summer?" he said. I looked at Amy and the water bubbling around her thighs, spraying her shorts. She looked at Mike, and I didn't want to surf anymore.

We said good-bye to my grandparents the following night. Mom backed her car out from their condominium and into the large asphalt parking lot for the adjacent marina. People walked their dogs there, sat on the benches, or fished in the bay. Seagulls flew above us in the fading light. We heard the rhythm of the brisk wind that blew freely over the open water. The metal shackles on the ropes chimed against the aluminum masts of sailboats.

"You kids never really told me about miniature golf yet," Mom said. "I know Katie had one more point than Jamie, but what else happened?"

"Amy got the ball in the clown's mouth at the end," Katie said. Her voice came faintly from the back seat. She pulled out the band keeping her hair in a ponytail and rested her head on the back of the seat. "None of us could do it."

"You sound tired, Katie," Mom said.

"We got ice cream after at the place next door," Katie said.

"Jamie, you gave Mike the money I sent you with, right?" Mom asked.

"No, Mom, he wouldn't take it."

"So he paid for miniature golf and ice cream? What a prince," Mom said. "Katie, don't you think he's handsome?"

But Katie didn't answer. At first I thought she just didn't want to respond, but when the headlights of the cars driving on the other side of the rode shone on her face, I saw that she was sleeping.

"She's out, Mom."

"What a lucky girl that Amy is. All those girls parading down the beach to see Mike and she gets him."

"She's not a girl, Mom."

"Oh you know what I mean. And even you can see what I'm saying about him, right? I mean he's nice to look at."

"Gross, Mom."

"Well, he is. And he's so good with you. We didn't have lifeguards like that when I was his age. I've told you about B. J., right?"

"Yes, you've talked about B.J., the guy who taught you how to sail."

"Now *he* was handsome. Not as tall as Mike, but he was charming, and he really knew how to sail."

"Mom, I'm tired," I said, pulling on the seat lever and leaning back.

"Do you think he'll marry Amy?"

"No."

"Why not?"

"She's too serious."

"Well, you can see that. She's probably smothering him. I probably would have too."

"I'm going to sleep," I said. The hull of a motorboat planed in the background, the propeller churning beyond the no-wake zone. Seagulls cried, sailboat masts pinged, and summer went on in Stone Harbor. Mom's wheels hummed over the road in the direction of Dad. I closed my eyes and was back underwater again, turning over, in forces stronger than myself. My arms stretched out toward Amy, my mother, and many miles past her to our house where my father sat in his wingback chair watching the news.

Overtime

—ɯ—

The kelly-green Eagles jersey flails over my head and around my arms like a hockey player who's losing a fight. Dad leans over me on my bed. I don't understand why he refuses to let me sleep in my game outfit. He grins as he pries the gray corduroys down from my waist. After he flings Ron Jaworski's number seven to the ground his wiry black eyebrows furrow and his mouth frowns. He puts his hands on his hips, and sighs as he leaves. You may recognize Jaworski—his nickname is Jaws—as one of ESPN's football analysts. Maybe Mom puts my pajamas on after. Maybe I cry. I'll be nine in two days. By refusing to let me wear my Eagles gear to bed, Dad violates our code, our unspoken truce about all things Eagles.

72

Overtime

I watch Jaws on TV as a boy, barking out signals from behind his narrow gray two-bar face mask. The Eagles suffer from a mighty hangover after their loss in New Orleans during Super Bowl XV. In 1981, they win ten games, but lose in the first round of the playoffs. The following season, the National Football League strike wipes out eight weeks of football, and, after a dismal year, the celebrated head coach Dick Vermeil resigns. In the following three seasons, when I'm ages seven, eight, and nine, the team's combined record is 18 wins, 29 losses, and 1 tie.

Apparently, these dire times are cause for calling upon Jesus, Mary, and Joseph for help. Or, actually, it sounds more like it is their fault, the way Dad pounds his fist on the arm of the chair and stalks by me, shaking the floorboards where I sit. When he calls upon the holy family, it sounds like "JeeeeeSUS MaryandJoseph," a long, overdramatic exhalation for the first syllable, and a breath in for the second. The Virgin Mary and the adopted father of the savior for the Christian religion are expelled in one collapsed grumble.

Those "Damn Birds" lose so often, I learn that part of the rules of the house mean toning down the chitchat during dinner after a defeat. If Dad raises an eyebrow at me, it is like a yellow flag on the field, a personal misconduct on my part. The eyebrow is worse than hearing him tell me to go sit in "the chair," my parents' '80s talk for taking a timeout. Mom and my sister can speak, and they have to carry the conversation. But if I blabber on it's a sign of blasphemy. Chirping at the table is disloyal—to the "Damn Birds" a little, but it's more about a bond we are forming over the Eagles. It is clear to me that Jaws is the leader. He gives the commands on the field and holds the

73

ball every play. I learn the rules of the game on the field and in the house. I learn to follow my dad's signals.

I am a few months away from making my First Communion. Each Sunday our family goes to nine o'clock Mass. After, my parents go out to breakfast with Grandma and Pop Pop, while my sister and I spend an hour in Confraternity of Catholic Doctrine class. Catholic kids who attend public school need to go to what is commonly referred to as CCD. I'm sure we talk about the Eucharist that fall. And at some point my conclusions cross disciplines.

During the prayers of the faithful at Mass, when the priest says, "And now for any intentions that lie in the silence of your hearts," I bow my head and pray for Jaws, and number eighty-two Mike Quick, possibly the most aptly named wide receiver in the history of the NFL.

The Eagles have the power to close any gaps between my father and me. I don't ever really question why it matters so much, but I accept Dad's prayerful bursts to the holy family as Eucharist. The team feeds our relationship. It is a subject of immediate and uncontested agreement between us. Touchdowns mean yelling, a shared grin, possibly a high five. An Eagles interception or a shanked field goal attempt mean calling upon Jesus Christ, or simply groaning incomprehensibly to each other as some constipated people tend to do privately.

I'm still trying to figure out why my father leaves before that game is over. It's just getting good, for the team and for us. In the first quarter the team mascot, Birdbrain, approaches our section. I run down to hand over my drawing of an Eagles helmet made with green, gray, and white pastel markers on yellow construction paper. I ask him to give it to Mike Quick. Birdbrain stops his frantic gestures for a moment. He points his beak in my dad's direction, then rubs my head with his wing, and moves along the metal railing waving white wings, knocking over empty clear plastic cups with oversize yellow bird feet.

The game is somewhat famous because of how it ends. The Eagles blow a seventeen-to-nothing lead. The Atlanta Falcons tie the game. They are twenty-five yards from the goal line. Nine seconds are left in the fourth quarter. They miss the field goal. In overtime, the red helmets receive the ball and cannot score. They punt it back to the home team. The punt soars in the air for sixty-two yards and dots the Eagles' five-yard line, bouncing out of bounds inside the one. The field position hushes the remaining sixty-three thousand fans who attend the game. We sit in section 372, row eleven. Maybe he makes us leave because of all the sloppy drunks, spilling beer and curses, as well as the thought of being in a post-game traffic jam with them and his only son. Or maybe it's that the game is in the opposite end zone. Without any warning, Dad pats both knees and says, "Let's go."

I descend concrete steps, and traverse through the concourse. Thousands upon thousands shift through the openings of each section entrance as we hustle past them. Each opening is a glimmer of where we were. The game is not over. And he decides to leave? It's overtime. Dad alters the lead shoulder under his blue jacket as he moves through the crowd. The back of his gray wool cap and the red flannel lining of his hood shift to the right, then the left. He is my lead blocker. The openings offer light, yellow security jackets, and traces of blue sky. The entrances are giant speakers amplifying a chant that is just catching on, or dying out. The public address announcer booms, and the crowd's thunderous murmur roars on.

In the car, Dad turns on the radio. Over the concrete and the steel, and up into the blue, all those voices erupt. Merrill Reese's voice crackles through the static side door speakers. "He's gonna go! 25-30, 35-40—midfield—45-40, 35-30. Mike Quick. Touchdown. The Eagles win." Jaws and Quick connect for an NFL record-tieing ninety-nine-yard touchdown pass, the winning score of the team's first overtime victory in franchise history. Dad's car wheels flatten a beer can. In my sideview mirror, I watch the aluminum slide and scrape the parking lot blacktop in the direction of the stadium—the concrete and the steel shrinking, as we drive away.

SUNDAY, SEPTEMBER 17, 2000
PHILADELPHIA EAGLES VS. GREEN BAY PACKERS

The 3–6 Eagles' loss is not the quarterback matchup it's hyped to be between gun-slinging Brett Favre and the scrambling second-year man, Donovan McNabb. It's a forgettable kicking contest between Ryan Longwell and David Akers, except that Dad visits me in Connecticut, and we watch it together. I stay in Connecticut after college, and sign up for a satellite service and the NFL package, which allows me to see every game, every Sunday.

Dad "cooks" before we leave for church. He cuts open a package of sauerkraut. The pickled cabbage and yellow juices squirt out of the bag and thud into the metal pot Dad has brought with him. He places three pieces of pork on a foundation of sauerkraut. Kielbasa, hot dogs, another bag of kraut and a bottle of beer fill the rest of the pot. Dad places the lid on top, turns the electric burner on low, rubs the palms of his hands together, and says, "Should be ready by kickoff."

The Eagles game is almost over. The pot on the stove is half empty. I shoot the TV with the remote to switch channels from one upcoming four o'clock game to the next. Dad sleeps in the La-Z-Boy. I sit a few feet away on the futon. The backs of his hands rest against his khaki-covered thighs. The fingers turn in toward the palms. The folds of his white-and-brown window-pane button-down shirt expand with his breath. Black glasses rest in his shirt pocket. Afternoon whiskers poke through his neck, lowered chin, and cheeks. His open mouth is pink. The wrinkles across his forehead cannot relax, even in sleep. Slow-motion replays and commercials shift colored lights between thin wisps of silver hairs on his shiny scalp.

I want him to wake up, raise his arms out toward the green players who flash on the screen with wings on their helmets. He should be hooting and hollering first names, in sentences punctuated by the pop of a single clap. I want his voice to bounce off my apartment walls, to grumble with me in disgust, to speak to me before he leaves.

SUNDAY, JANUARY 18, 2008
PHILADELPHIA EAGLES VS. ARIZONA CARDINALS

When the crisp air of autumn returns, and maple leaves crunch underfoot, watching football can be as holy for me as praying in church. I manage to bring my Sunday bachelor practice and the NFL satellite package into family life. We lay on top of green pillows, the floor, the couch, and each other. We take turns holding James, who's almost four months old. He wears the same kelly-green sweatshirt with gray snaps that was once mine. The Eagles' patch on the chest is separating from the cotton. The gray strings from the hood have frayed. I guess in the mid-seventies, when the sweatshirt was made, they actually made baby clothing with strings.

Lynne ladles her chili into bread bowls before the one o'clock games, and, by the four o'clock kickoff, she'll slide a tray of tortilla chips topped with her chili, chopped raw onions, and shredded cheddar cheese out of the top metal rack of the oven. James will nap in his crib, while Lynne sleeps on the couch. It's our day of rest.

Sundays become as dead as my father when the Philadelphia Eagles' season ends. The whistles, cheers, replays, and familiar commercials we may have grown to like—it all recedes into a winter snowstorm and hibernates for eight months.

I throw the remote across the room that January night. It bounces off the couch. Batteries and plastic pieces clatter across the carpet as midnight green jerseys head for the locker-room and the off-season. The wings arched in mid-flap on the players' helmets walk past white-and-cardinal red jerseys celebrating their National Football Conference Championship victory and a trip to Tampa, Florida, to face the Pittsburgh Steelers in Super Bowl XLIII. A haze of red and white confetti litters the TV screen.

Without the relevance, the immediacy of the game, or the promise of the next game, the paraphernalia surrounding me seems lifeless. The kelly green and the midnight green constitute the colors of my dual self; the son who longs for his dad and the young man who, in 1999 (when the uniform changed to midnight green), prepares to graduate college and find a job—to grow up. Midnight green fades through red and white confetti like the faces of people walking outside when the flakes fall and winter gusts blow white everywhere. The team's fourth NFC Championship game loss in seven years sends me into a fury, an illogical frenzy my wife of two and a half years hasn't seen yet because I've been too embarrassed to unleash myself fully over those Damn Birds.

I have yet to consider ridding myself of this ridiculous obsession, but I do want to tear down the posters, autographed pictures, football cards, the three helmets on the shelf, and the deflated football, cracked and autographed by the entire 1988 team. McNabb and the Damn Birds have brought me too close, too many times. The remaining au jus and roast beef steaming in clouds above the Crock-Pot nauseates me. My barley-and-hops-soaked head throbs.

What do I expect from a Super Bowl victory? A championship team cannot grant me the transfiguration of my father. It wouldn't deliver him from the subconscious to a seat on the couch for an introduction to his daughter-in-law and his grandson. It wouldn't give us the chance to talk again, or exchange a grin. Football cannot resurrect a father.

Most of the players that stare back at me through dusty glass frames are retired. I call out their names next to Dad, as a kid. Some of them aren't even alive anymore. And when that season ended, when every season ends, the room haunts me until the sting of the playoff loss wears off. The Eagles' wall clock ticks above the TV. The once-white pennants spanning three decades seem to yellow before my eyes. The 1960 NFL Championship team poster did not belong to me. They have never been my team. They're stories of a famed past, names from another century: Norm Van Brocklin, Tommy McDonald, and Chuck Bednarik—the players who beat Vince Lombardi's Green Bay Packers at Franklin Field are ghosts of Sundays long ago.

And why do I hang my childhood poster of football helmets? The NFL consisted of twenty-eight teams then. The images occupied my boyhood mind at night. In the weeks leading up to Christmas, I left the Advent candles on in my bedroom. They were single plastic candles, with a bulb for a flame. The lights illuminated the helmets, my parents were in the next room, and I was free to wonder: *Can I name the state where each team is located? Is it the name of the capital city? If not, what is the capital city? Can I name who is in first place in each division? Can I connect the Eagles helmet to the one belonging to their opponent this week in horizontal, vertical, or diagonal lines? Darn. What about next week? Wait. Who are we playing next Sunday? Maybe I can guess?*

I shouldn't expect old faces and variations of green to reconnect me to my dead father. Perhaps I've surrounded myself with autographed football cards of Ron Jaworski, Harold Carmichael, Wilbert Montgomery, and Mike Quick, those stars of the early '80s, to hear their names spoken in my father's voice, to hear his voice once again holler at the TV with mine when the game is on and the collective voices of thousands hums through the TV speakers. My grief is not the loss on the field, but the loss of the man, whose absence makes off-season Sundays as empty as Veterans Stadium moments before it imploded.

Overtime

I spread the Eagles blanket out on the floor and put all three helmets in the middle: the midnight-green helmet with white wings, the kelly-green one with gray wings, and the mini white helmet with green wings. I wear my father's gray T-shirt, which he bought at Lehigh University during training camp in 2000. McNabb was a rookie then. I reached out to shake his hand in the autograph tent that morning and shot him an awkward grin when his large hand enveloped mine and his fingers wrapped around my wrist and part of my forearm.

I form an X with both arms, grab the bottom and fling the worn cotton of the T-shirt onto the helmets. James sits on the floor and watches me. I unsnap his sweatshirt and pull it off. I hold the blanket together at the corners and head upstairs. I ransack my drawers, and continue to fill the blanket with Eagles apparel.

In the attic, I shove it all in the bin of summer clothes. I hammer the plastic lid with my fist, and ask myself, "Why should this loss drive me to stand, shirtless, panting alone in the dusty cold attic on a dark winter's night?" When Dad was alive, as I grew older, I vowed to keep football in perspective, to recover from a loss and engage others at the dinner table. And yet, this is how he would have reacted—stunned into silent anger. Dad shakes his head in my memory, and I shake mine back at him. *Get a grip. Dad,* I think to myself. But here I am in the attic.

SUNDAY, NOVEMBER 1, 2009
NEW YORK GIANTS VS. PHILADELPHIA EAGLES

I know football games are an excuse to melt cheese on tortilla chips, drink a beer in the afternoon, and hang out. At thirteen months old, I teach James to lift his arms toward the brown wood panels of the ceiling and say, "Touch, touch, touch," whenever the Eagles cross the goal line. And I know that I'm seducing him by buying him gear and wrapping him up in excessive affection when he raises both arms. I have sold it to Lynne as our day of rest. I turn the volume down late in the afternoon while she naps on the couch.

The leaves on the limbs of my neighbor's birch tree blanket the yard in an autumn quilt. The Eagles on the walls in my den hover through memory, awakening my younger self. The team is off to a promising four-win and two-loss start. McNabb has passed the ball well, and speedy, young, skill players LeSean McCoy, DeSean Jackson, and Jeremy Maclin dash across the screen for big plays.

But even casual fans know McNabb doesn't have many good years left in his career. And soon, someone my father and I never watched together will replace him as the next franchise quarterback.

My father eludes me in the commotion of every day. I walk on the 300-level concourse of a stadium that no longer exists. I thought that as I grew older, the fanaticism might wear off, dwindle at least into a controlled following, with a more grounded emotional response to the outcomes of Eagles games. But what has remained, if not intensified, is a feeling—an old hope rises up that the winged helmets can once again close the gap between us. Under the wood-paneled ceiling, and between the sage green walls, while I recline in my chair in the reverie of a lazy Sunday, catching my father seems possible, if only he would turn around.

Injury Report:
August 16, 2001

—ɯ—

On August 15, 2001, Philadelphia Eagles' left defensive tackle
Corey Simon (head) was a limited participant in practice after
sustaining a concussion six days before. Simon, a twenty-four-
year-old first-round draft pick out of Florida State, later said he
remembered fighting off a double team and then colliding with
a running back. As the fans in the aluminum bleachers watched,
trainers went to work immobilizing Simon's head. All eighty-
four other players stopped what they were doing, and so did
the coaches. Some players rested on one knee. A few linemen
breathed through oxygen masks. Others let assistants squeeze
water into their mouths. Some who claimed to have seen the
play recounted what they saw. Meanwhile, the thousands of

fans in the aluminum bleachers waited to see Simon get up. Yes, they loved the grace of Donovan McNabb's touchdown pass, which arced over the arms and heads of defensive backs to land in James Thrash's hands—that made them clap and cheer—but these football fans drove hours to the team's training camp site at Lehigh University in Bethlehem, Pennsylvania, because they wanted to see these massive men endure what they couldn't see coming, what knocked them down. The thousands in the bleachers wanted to see Simon get up, to see him stand.

Before Jim Chesbro's heart attack and the emergency quadruple bypass surgery on August 2, Jim had planned to take his twenty-four-year-old son to Lehigh University to see the Eagles practice on the final day of training camp, on August 16.

On August 15, however, while Corey Simon took himself out of contact drills during the afternoon practice, Jim Chesbro could only walk for two minutes in the backyard, even though the doctors had advised him to walk for five minutes each day. The humidity made it hard for him to breathe. Perspiration dotted the pale skin around Jim's temples and above his gray eyebrows. His son gave him water and helped him untie his white sneakers while Jim sat, trying to catch his breath, on the hospital bed he rented in the house he had rented since the divorce.

The next morning, before the Eagles began their practice on the last day of training camp, as fans began arriving in Bethlehem, Jim told his son to call 911. That day James Thrash caught more passes from McNabb, one of them for a long gain. During another play, rookie running back Correll Buckhalter made an impressive block, jumping in front of the full-speed blitz of a linebacker. Meanwhile, Corey Simon (head) remained a limited participant.

On this final day of training camp, the Eagles did not report any major injuries, but Jim could not catch his breath. The police officer was the first to arrive. He placed an oxygen mask over Jim's mouth, but it didn't help. Later, doctors determined that Jim had suffered a pulmonary failure. His lungs were bleeding, which was why it was hard for him to speak between heaves.

That season, Jim's son watched Corey Simon start all sixteen regular season games, and record thirty-six tackles. Since then, Jim's son has told his cardiologist about the sporadic stings and random pangs in his chest, but tests reveal no sign of injury. Every August, while National Football League training camps take place, Jim's son sits across from his cardiologist for his annual appointment. Before leaving, he stands, and the doctor assures him he's fine.

Rip Van Father

—w—

Sunlight shines through the windows on the floor in squares and rectangles. It shines on the metal legs of the desks in my empty classroom. I'm reading "Rip Van Winkle" again, trying to think of an interesting entry point for the students. When I wasn't much older than the seventeen-year-old boys whom I teach, my father was grilling me about my studies in college, about grades, and the cost of tuition. He asked me if I had read "Rip Van Winkle" by Washington Irving in any of my literature courses.

When I admitted that I hadn't, and my not-yet old man realized he had one on me, he leaned into the steering wheel, slapping his thigh. "Seriously, you haven't read 'Rip Van Winkle?'" he said. "Geez what am I paying for, anyway?"

The freshman football players no longer chatter while waiting for their bus on the sidewalk below. Their cleats no longer clack as they walk. By now their footballs are thudding on the field at a school miles from here. The squeaking brakes and honking horns of after-school traffic are silenced. The young boys who want everyone to see them driving have left. They rode away with their windows down and the music so loud their parents' cars rattled.

White seagulls circle outside my second-floor window as I reconsider how to analyze the tone Irving creates in the humorous tale. The gulls hover on the breeze with their wings spread, soaring over the parking lot. Leaves perform their annual stunt. They shine autumn orange, red, and brown, and their skins reflect the promise of an evening sky. The prep school where I teach is on the far side of the campus and from my window, I see the university buildings—the roof of the recreational complex, the campus center, the science building—and above them all, the trees. On the other side of the large oaks are the chapel and the mansion where Jim, the Jesuit priest, is probably still working in his office. Behind the mansion is the large, flat green field where I graduated. You can see the blue waters of the Long Island Sound from this field, and this is where I picture my father standing with me after my graduation ceremony. It was one of the last times he visited me, the last time he was here, where I live. And while I'm trying to read the story in the thin pages of my anthology, the black ink merges into a large blur, and my eyes return to the windows and the trees and the image of my father standing next to me in my cap and gown.

I used to read the story and wonder why my father liked it so much. Did the story stand out in his mind because of the way Dame Van Winkle is characterized, as a "termagant wife" and "a tolerable blessing; and if so, Rip Van Winkle was thrice blessed." Would that line have cracked him up if he had a chance to read it again? I bet Rip's dog, Wolf, would have reminded him of his Siberian husky, who died when I was young. How my father probably longed for his old companion after his wife declared divorce, and how he would have loved to drink from Rip Van Winkle's flagon. No more legal bills, mortgages, car loans, or college tuition for his two teenage children hanging over his head. No checks to write for rent and alimony. How Dad would have loved to leave the divorce proceedings with Dame Chesbro for the forest, with his old Siberian husky trotting by his side, wagging his big fluffy tail.

I used to think the story drew me in because I wish my father could return after all this time, as Rip returns after a two-decade-long sleep in the Catskill Mountains. And like Rip's daughter, I wish I could find my father in the midst of a crowd in my town and take him home where he could live with us.

As I look out the windows, I imagine my father standing next to me as we did on the day of my graduation. I had found a stump and I stepped upon it so that I appeared taller than him. All this time, while the Long Island Sound flows beyond the green lawn and the classroom where I teach, my father has evolved within me. He died before ever having an e-mail address, before text messages and touch-screen smartphones. He died before Starbucks seemed to be in every town. He died three weeks before the Twin Towers burned and fell.

I'm looking out my windows at the tall oaks shimmering in the breeze. I've been trying to arrive on the other side of those trees to find my father. I imagine charging through the wooded areas of campus between where I sit and the lawn where we stood next to each other. I trample the sticks and leaves, and scatter squirrels, deer, sparrows, and cardinals. I have been barging into my memory to find my father ever since he died, swatting away branches, banging off trunks, and charging forward.

Each year, a new version of myself emerges, and we all run together. These versions of myself speak to one another. They speak of where we've seen him before. "Dad," we shout. "Dad." We tell each other he is just up ahead. There are five of us in our thirties. We bring up the rear and care for the youngest ones. Sometimes the toddlers are confused and think we are him.

And sometimes the older ones give in to grief and lament to one another, "Nobody knows Jim Chesbro in Connecticut." Eventually, though, one of us declares, "But we do. We know our father."

A boy running in front of us wears an Eagles helmet and carries a football in his arm, pressed against his ribs. The helmet falls over his face and he lifts the two-bar face mask so he can see. Another wears a canvas bag carrying newspapers. He adjusts the strap every other step, and when I ask him if I can carry it for him, he gives me a straight-arm and balks. "I can do it," he says.

I find an altar boy on his knees off on the right flank. He blesses himself, presses his palms together, and mumbles. I lift him to his feet and tell him to run. He says he's praying, and I tell him that running is our prayer. He has no idea what I mean. "Rise and run," I say.

The guys in their middle twenties are jerks to everyone else. No one really talks to them. We understand they have a lot to be angry about. We know his last breaths haunt them. The groom dashes forth, the coattails of his tux draping his backside as he jogs. The teens follow him everywhere and he tells them about Lynne and their hope for children. I watch them all scatter leaves as they run in front of me, talking to each other—breathing. I watch them, knowing I have to return, knowing I will hear their voices after I close my book.

Flakes In The Mane

If I write of hiking up a mountain with my one-year-old boy riding like a papoose on my back, and of what he babbled to me while we gazed down from the summit onto the scudding clouds, it is not because I am deluded into believing that my baby, like the offspring of Prince Charles, matters to the great world. It is because I know the great world produces babies of its own and watches them change cloud-fast before its doting eyes. To make that climb up the mountain vividly present for readers is harder work than the climb itself. I choose to write about my experience not because it is mine, but because it seems to me a door through which others might pass.

—SCOTT RUSSELL SANDERS

Night Running

—⚋—

I like to run down the main avenue two blocks from our house. The thoroughfare is a border between the town where we live and the town where we'd like to live. A few other joggers and bikers are out in the deep blue and purple of twilight. Maybe they're coming home from work late, and this is their only time to exercise. Or perhaps they are embarrassed by the way they look in their running apparel. Do they fear drivers, walkers, or bikers observing the strain in their faces, their backs and heads giving way to gravity and exhaustion? Are they trying to hide their vulnerability as much as I am?

Under the veil of dusk, I project my insecurities onto my neighbors without them seeing me shake my head, or shoot judgmental looks through their windows and front doors. I start by walking parallel to the double yellow lines on our street.

Night Running

There are nine residences on our end of the block. We all own our homes.

The renters who populate the rest of our street are indifferent to the appearance of the property they inhabit. They are as careless with each other as they are with the trash they leave on the ground. One tenant drives a Mack truck for a living. He rumbles down the street sounding his truck horn when he returns, regardless of the hour. Most other moments of the night and day, the entire block can hear him and his wife yelling and cursing.

In my twenties, I lived in a different neighborhood. My roommate and I rented the first floor from Mrs. B., who lived above us. During our five years there, we mowed the lawn, trimmed the hedges, and swept the front porch. We sat on the furniture we had from our college days and watched ESPN. We went to bars. In the morning, beyond the ledge of the front porch, when the low angle of the sun and the steaming cup of coffee in our hands woke us up to the uncertainty of our relationships to women who did not become our wives (and careers we were not sure we wanted), at least the yard was in order.

I walk faster past multifamily houses that have as many as three addresses and mailboxes posted around the front doors. Crabgrass spreads over old broken concrete. The feathered blades reach out onto the cracked slabs worn down by the steady stream of occupants. I step into a trot. Stones and pieces of cement grind against the rubber tread of my sneakers. Debris overflows from the renters' trash cans and is left to rot in the weeds and dirt patches beside the crumbling curb. I watch for cars as they slide through the stop signs at the end of the street. I allow a woman with a flashlight and a German shepherd to cross the intersection before me. A circle of light jostles back and forth on the sidewalk in front of her, and the dog's tag *clink, clink, clink, clinks* in rhythm with their hurried pace.

After running a few blocks down the avenue, I turn left and ascend the street that separates the first two holes from the remaining front nine of a country club's prized old New England golf course. I like to run under these tall oak trees. Their wide trunks bifurcate into branches of swaying leaves. I like to run on the uneven blacktop sidewalk. I know this path. I can anticipate dips and cracks underfoot. I like to run in the dark, because this way the people who live here can't see me trying so hard. They can't see me pushing. They can't see me sweating. They can't see me panting. They can't see how much I want our family to live here. Headlights cast my silhouette on the bark of trees, lining the fairway like columns. The profile runs on tree after tree. I'd like to think I can catch the shadow of myself at the top of the hill, where the sky opens up to a full silver moon, but when I am there my shadow is gone. Airplane lights flash red, avoiding each other in the black air traffic.

I make a right, crossing over sticks, leaves, and road sediment. I run down the winding road and past an elementary school. My wife and I would like our son to go here in four years. We have one car. We're sharing it for one year. We're saving up. The sacrifice is most stressful in the morning, even though my wife and I work at the same high school. Our son, James, is two years old. We load the car with James's mini-cooler of food and sippy-cups for daycare.

I run at night so I can leave our house and return at my own pace.

Night Running

I make another right turn while running in the middle of the road under the glow of streetlights. A pregnant mother carries her toddler in one arm and her purse in the other. The boy could be James's age. They walk down the slate pathway toward their sport wagon. The stately, black front door of their home looms in the background over their heads. Another mother walks out of a nearby house with her son. He wears a mesh football jersey and baseball cap. He walks with the nonchalance of a nine-year-old. Their laughs and good-bye pleasantries drift through the air and echo down the street over the incessant chirping of crickets. They walk across the street, and their neighbor's porch swing rocks in the shadows of the glass-paneled brass lantern hanging above the screen door. I hear crickets and the *pat, pat, pat, pat* of my rubber-soled footsteps landing on the smooth asphalt.

So much is at stake during one's thirties. Most adults have a sense of who they are, and a vision for where they'd like to be. They understand that moving up in their careers or to a new home will take time, planning, effort, and opportunity. As much as I wish I could speed up this process of advancing, I know I cannot. So I take to the road at night, because I can control my running pace. I can look into the big windows and see families sitting down to a late dinner, or watching TV together. I like to run by each house and pretend I could make an offer. I look for any flaw I could share with my real estate agent to bring to the negotiation. I don't find any in the dark. Perhaps the veil under which I hide myself has put a glossy film over my vision.

I imagine what the interior of one of these places would look like with my family in it. James's room would have a sports theme. I picture him as a seven-year-old. He shoots his Nerf basketball until I walk in and tell him it's time to hit the sack. To my surprise, when I picture our master bedroom, it looks the same as the one we have. The room is a muted light green, with clean white molding. The wood of the vaulted ceiling's beams matches the furniture and is darker than the hardwood floor.

I return my eyes to the road in front of me and think about how our family is a few years away from putting our house on the market. Even though this street doesn't have any Mack trucks parked on it, I'm sure that in the light of day it isn't as perfect as it seems during my night running. Maybe this is one of the reasons I keep running at night. These houses appear perfect. Perhaps this is the most dangerous part of night running.

Is it the influence of our American culture that makes me think I should know where I'll be in ten years, or is it just my personality? Why am I in such a hurry? I cannot supersede the law of progress, or speed up the development of my skills. I cannot learn from the writers and editors I have yet to meet. I cannot learn from the books I have yet to read. I cannot write today what I will experience tomorrow. I cannot interview for the positions that are not yet available.

So I run. I run in the middle of the road to the night music of crickets. I run through the quiet side streets back to the main road. I run parallel to the double yellow lines, anticipating ruts and bumps in the asphalt sidewalk because I know this path. The avenue is not as populated as before the sun went down. The rich hues of twilight have long given way to darkness. I run down blocks of parked cars and sleeping children. Lights from televisions flash in the windows. Headlights pass and illuminate the bend in the street. They shine in the direction of our house.

I always run faster on the way back. I sprint the last two blocks until I reach our driveway. The green grass is edged along the hourglass-shaped sidewalk that leads to the lights on either side of the door, which I painted burgundy. The lights shine onto the beige siding and black shutters I installed. I lean over my shorts breathing hard. A little girl's handprint is next to my foot on the concrete slab. Her name is Nikki. I brushed white paint over the growth chart her parents must have penciled onto the closet door in James's room. In the next concrete slab, Lynne and I left our handprints in the year we married. I hired a crew to install a new sidewalk slab, the entire curb, and the asphalt driveway. The driveway lights reflect off our windows. I had every one replaced before James was born.

Lynne is inside preparing lunches for the next day. She is opening and closing the cabinets we painted white. We've painted every room in this house. James asks Lynne for more milk. I expected that he would be asleep by now. I thought I would walk into his room, and find him rolled over onto his side, his knees tucked into his chest, a comfort blanket pushed up against his face, his big tired breaths audible over the humming air filter. I climb the brick steps of the side entrance, open the door, and walk into the well-lit kitchen of our home. I can see our family, standing where we are.

In the Paper Route of My Mind

—ɯ—

One woman still moves in the paper route of my mind. I see her when I'm loading the car with my laptop bag, and James's mini-cooler for day care. She shuffles out of my memory in the morning, in the form of my neighbor who lives in the house across the street.

I first saw her on Easter morning, my first day of my first job. My father had helped me fold the thick Sunday editions in half. He resisted the urge to snap at me like the bands we placed around the papers. I had thrown them in the canvas bag, anxious to see if I could carry them all and ride my bike. "No. No. No," he said. "Not like that. They won't all fit. Like this," he said, placing them upright.

In the Paper Route of My Mind

I straddled my bike in the backyard, and rammed the gate open with my front tire. The wood scraped the concrete driveway as the door swung open. Dad sat behind the wheel of his idling white Buick.

He leaned his head out the window and said, "I can drive you." I rode past the car to the canvas bag. Dad remained in the driver's seat. His head rested in his hand. News radio played through his open window. My feet left the brick sidewalk, and pedaled one slow rotation before the canvas bag with the *Courier Post* printed on the side in orange block letters broke my fall.

"C'mon, son" he said, as the motor hummed and the timing belts turned. I flung the strap off of my neck and planned on placing each one in the back seat. But Dad was already upon me, and he shouldered the bag and shoved it in the grand bench-like front seat.

My father's red brake lights flashed ahead of me through our neighborhood. He held a newspaper out the window of his car. As I turned to run to the next house I saw the robed woman with rollers in her hair. She had walked to the curb and waved.

During the week I did not need my father to help me deliver the small bundles I sent flying end over end. The wheels of my bike bumped over the breaks in the slabs of sidewalk as the thin editions bounced on wraparound porches and front steps, sounding like the cardboard cylinder of a roll of paper towels hitting the kitchen floor.

When I strap James into his car seat, the plastic clip clicks, and sometimes the woman across the street bends carefully at the waist to pick up what I assume is the *Connecticut Post*. She does not wave. Cars scatter leaves to the curbs of our busy street. Red brake lights flash at the intersection, and none of them are my father's.

From the Rust and Sawdust

—ɯ—

1.

The rim was cracked. The brown and red writing had faded on the old white mug that said Dad with a capital D. My sister and I had given it to him for Father's Day when we were kids. I thought drinking from it would be a way to have a cup of coffee with my father in the morning, but the crack irritated my mouth. The coffee tasted bitter. I felt like a fraud. I'm not my father. This was his mug. And he's dead.

2.

Eleven steps led up to the attic of my house. I shimmied my father's old bookcase through the doorway. My hands reached around to the sides, but couldn't find a grip. My fingers slid up and down the wood that he had painted white. I stood next to the damn thing and grabbed hold of a shelf. *Bang*. First step. *Bang*. Second step. I turned my palm up, wedged my bent arm into the opening of one of the five shelves, and bore the brunt of the weight on one shoulder. Standing on the attic floorboards, I considered lowering my shoulder and tipping it over. I leaned on my knees with stiff arms instead. The bookshelf was my offering to the graveyard of cardboard boxes. Disturbed dust particles descended in the light, landing on the duct tape and permanent black marker in thin layers. The cobwebs connecting the boxes wavered in the shifting air of the unfinished attic.

I'm old enough to wonder which art and photography books were his favorites. What did he turn to for inspiration as a sketch artist, or as a teacher? We were friends when he died. I would have asked him, eventually, if we had had more time.

3.

In the black-and-white photograph, my father stands in his classroom holding a camera. I had kept the framed image in my own classroom for a while. I was throwing a foam football around to generate discussion with my students, and one of them tossed the ball too low, and it hit the frame on my desk and broke the glass. In the picture, four of my father's students sit on stools along a rectangular table. Three heads bend down, and over my father's shoulder, one of his students looks out the windows of the room, and it's hard not to presume his imagination was at work.

After the frame broke, a fine, one-inch line scarred my father's chest, above his heart. His right hand grips the top of the camera. His left is turned under. His thumb, middle, ring, and pinky fingers cup the lens. He is wearing his ring and a watch. His hairy arms are exposed in his sleeveless, button-down shirt. The collar is open at the top. His lips are parted, as if he is about to speak. The smile lines around his mouth are ready to press into action. Black-framed glasses rest on the bridge of his nose. His eyes stare out over them, into the camera and, I like to think, at me.

4.

The desktop was five feet long and over two feet wide. The wood was dull beige, hard and heavy, fortified with some industrial synthetic resin. I could see a reflection of myself on its shiny surface. After my father died, I moved it out of his house in New Jersey to my apartment in Connecticut. In the years the desktop spent in Dad's classroom, the house he rented, my two apartments, and the house I bought, not a scratch, dent, or nick marred its surface. I drilled the first, second, and third long, thick screws out. The fourth jammed. I tipped the desk on its side. The wood creaked. I wrenched free the two drawers with both hands.

I carried the desktop down the stairs, avoiding walls and moldings. I lifted it over my head and slid it over the metal ridge of the dumpster. The walls echoed behind me as I walked to the garage in pursuit of a sledgehammer.

Old kitchen chairs, a mattress, an air-conditioner, clothes, shoes, and pieces of Dad's orange wingback chair shifted under the report of the metal sledgehammer head. The mismatched décor of college leftovers and Dad's old furniture had filled the empty space in the apartment I shared with my best friend.

The stubborn desktop broke into parts under my feet, and I repositioned myself after each blow. I pounded the desktop until the parts splintered and cracked. Broken fragments bounced into the air over torn wood fibers.

5.

The tailor removed material from the back and then the bottom of my father's black overcoat. The sleeves came to my wrist, the bottom of the black wool draped around my knees. The shoulders, however, were big—linebacker-shoulder-pads big. I looked as if I was equipped to shrug my shoulders, cast the coat to the ground on the sidelines, strap on a helmet, and enter a football game. I looked as though I was wearing my father's coat.

6.

The brass base and neck of the desk lamp extended to a ceramic green oval shade. While painting a model airplane at my childhood desk, my father loved to walk in, turn on the lamp over my head, and say, "Why don't you shed some light on the subject?" I don't need to keep his desk lamp to remember him saying this corny line to me. After seeing this same lamp at an office supply store on sale for $14.99, I trashed it. I'm not discarding my father. I'm chucking a cheap lamp.

7.

Three pairs of my father's wool slacks hang in a plastic zipper bag in the same closet as our coats by the front door of our home.

8.

I like the blue-green and black plaid with red and yellow inter-secting lines on his wool tie. My students sometimes say they have the same tie. And I tell them my grandparents bought it in Scotland for their son-in-law over thirty years ago. My wife says it looks like her Catholic grammar school skirt. If I am in defense of prolonging a memory, a picture in my mind of my father in a blue blazer and charcoal slacks at Christmas, then why do I wear it? I tell myself his fingers slid along the red and yellow lines, that the wool brushed against his buttons when he breathed. I loosen the Windsor knot around my neck after the last bell of my teaching day, and it's a relief to remember, in a moment between the students' voices emptying from my classroom and echoing against the metal lockers, and before the announcements thunder through the ceiling speaker, that I belong to him too.

9.

I imagine the blank board in my father's hands when he was a student a student at the University of the Arts. He probably brushed the dark stain into the grain first, and then painted the white border. Every line of the flags of the International Code of Signals remains straight and even. He must have drawn and then painted flags alpha to zulu; pennant one through zero; and the club flags, first, second, and third substitutes. Some brush strokes are perpendicular, but most run parallel with the grain. The rope wraps around the border of the board and is tied in a knot. On top of my father's old dresser, I edit my writing, under lamplight and the International Code of Signals.

10.

Three sets of colored pencils remain in the box that sits on my bookshelf in my home office. My father gave me five boxes of colored pencils and a stack of drawing paper. "Here," he said one day when I was with him in his art classroom, "Use 'em for projects." And I did. My freshmen broke them. I found them on the floor between the metal desk legs. But I don't teach freshmen anymore and I've never had the courage to ask the upperclassmen to illustrate the scenes we study.

My son can hold crayons, markers, pens, and pencils between his index finger and thumb. He likes to rotate his hand and watch the color appear on the page in overlapping lines. I give him a box of colored pencils. He draws green, red, blue, yellow, and black circles on the drawing paper. James doesn't know they are from his grandfather. I'm not saddened when they snap, when the lead color flies out from between each of his fists. I give him more pencils so he can draw circles. I wonder if he is holding what his grandfather held, if the real gift is not the pencils, but in the discovery, that one day James will hold up a piece of paper and say, "Look!" And we will see in the unbroken lines that he can draw.

11.

From the rust and sawdust at the bottom of his metal toolbox, I lifted a white pencil with *'81 Buick* printed in red. Below the Buick logo, an eagle spread its wings across the pencil. As I examined the details between the dull lead point and the worn pink eraser, I heard my father say, "Whatever you do, I don't want you going into the car business." We were in his car. I had just told him my plans to major in English and that I was thinking about becoming a teacher. *I'm following in your footsteps, Dad,* I thought as I said it. *You're flattered, right? Don't become a car salesman? Dad, I said, teacher. I'm going to teach high school English.*

As I rolled the wood between my pointer finger and thumb, the memory in the car unfolded. Dad had more to say, but not much. "Can you imagine where I'd be now if I quit teaching and accepted your grandfather's offer to sell cars full-time?" he said.

I didn't want to sell cars and I was never invited to do so.

"Why not, Dad?" I simply asked.

"Just promise me. All right? You can do better," he said. "You really want to be a teacher, huh?"

"Yeah, I like my English courses. The long papers intimidate the hell out of me, but once I get started, I actually like thinking about the characters and all that."

"Well, it's better than selling cars."

Every time he looked for a screwdriver, hammer, or drill bit and flicked the pencil out of the way, my father made a decision not to throw it out. Every September he walked into room A-10 and his vocation as an art teacher. The white pencil is a relic, a reminder in the back of my office desk drawer, of what is worth keeping.

12.

My father's cotton and flannel plaid shirts hang in James's closet. I bring them to my face in hopes of detecting the familiar trace of his musty house and Zest soap. The sleeves brush against each other when I free one of my own shirts from its metal hanger. They all hang together, like formless arms shifting enough to sway back and forth, as if they deliver a single wave to the dust on the floor.

On the other side of the closet wall is Mary's room. After Mary falls asleep and before James gives up on prolonging his bedtime routine, he runs around his bed and into his closet. I chase after him. He giggles and climbs on his hamper. I grab him with both hands under his arms. My fingers press into the fleece pajamas around his torso. Through the faint light from the hallway, he reaches for his grandfather's shirtsleeves, pulling him toward us.

13.

I had his white plastic laundry basket. It stayed in the rotation for seven years, until the day the crack on one of the side handles scratched my arm. I walked down the driveway, lifted the lid on the trash can, and dropped it in. The white plastic echoed in the large green container. I don't think my father would want me to be weighed down by his stuff. Each time I throw out a mug or a lamp that was his, I am lighter. He did not raise me to hoard his old junk and pretend to be him. He raised me to put out my hand, look someone in the eye, and introduce myself with the name he gave me.

Like a
Lion in the Snow

—ᴍ—

When my wife and I were expecting our second child, during a snowstorm, I envisioned a lion walking to me up the street. I watched him from our bay window as he trotted along the middle of the road. He squinted his eyes against the cascading sheets of white blowing his shaggy mane. He pawed up our sidewalk, driveway, and front steps. The lion turned to face the street. He rested on his hindquarters, yawned toward the sky, and expelled a fog of hot breath into the falling flakes, before collapsing his massive head on his front legs.

I am not prone to visits from imaginary animals. The first time I pictured him in the snow, the beast terrified me. I hadn't seen the movie *Gladiator* in a long time, nor had I watched any African wildlife shows on the National Geographic channel. Was I afraid fathering two children would consume me, as lions once consumed Christians? Once the lion turned toward the street, yawned, and rested his head, he reminded me of the lion statues guarding the entryways of palaces. Why did I have these daydreams?

The first lions arrived at America's oldest zoo, in Philadelphia, shortly after it opened, in 1874. When my parents brought me to the Philadelphia Zoo a little over one hundred years later, there were two, a male and female, named Pierre and Elsa. In the grainy picture I found from that visit, my father stands behind me, his hands gripping the metal handle of the stroller in front of an exhibit of elephants. The grass is burnt the color of straw and my father's arms are deeply tanned. I was two years old at the time, and while examining the photograph it occurs to me that this was most likely the first time I heard the sounds of an African lion in person. If Pierre's roar did reverberate through my two-year-old frame that day, then this visit to the zoo becomes the origin of my awe for the male African lion. A lion's roar travels nearly five miles, which makes me think I must have heard Pierre roar at least once that day.

How does a two-year-old make sense of such a fear-inducing sensation? I don't count hearing the sounds of an African lion through electronic transmissions—like, for example, the roar of MGM's Leo the Lion playing through the speakers of a television (Leo spent his retirement at the Philadelphia Zoo, by the way, from 1931 to 1935). Hearing a lion roar, growl, woof, and rumble *in person* is a sensation that you not only hear with your ears, but *feel* with your body.

One summer day after our son was born, my uncle invited me to play golf with him as his guest at the Stone Harbor Golf Club. The eleventh fairway at my uncle's club just so happened to be adjacent to the driveway of the Cape May County Zoo, where Brutu, an older male lion who was known for his habitual roaring, lived. The only thing I remember about playing there with Uncle Clark were Brutu's sounds. I don't remember where my tee shot landed, only the sound waves of the apex predator's roars reaching my body before I began my back swing. Hearing a lion roar seems more distracting than seeing an alligator sunbathing near a water hazard, as they often do on many Floridian courses. As I took one more glance at the fairway before I pulled the clubhead back, I envisioned Brutu standing in the fairway, his jaws open, roaring at me. His roar penetrated my senses, followed by deep guttural woofs floating around us, like the humid oceanic air drifting onshore from the bay.

During Lynne's second trimester with our second child, one evening in March while it snowed, I saw the lion again. My wife sat on the couch with both hands on her belly. I watched the flakes appear in the streetlight. If I allow myself to continue to visualize the lion on my front steps, he snarls. He shakes off the flakes in his mane, the wind blowing the black and brown fur. He bares his teeth. A low rumbling sound from deep within his five-hundred-pound body becomes a roar. His head is nearly level with mine as I stand beside the bay window and imagine this lion's presence outside my front door.

"Come here," she said.

Our son was sleeping in his crib. The house was quiet. I removed my hands from my pockets and placed them on her belly.

"Feel that?" she asked.

I stood over her and stared at the rug on the floor, thinking about the lion, as Lynne watched my face. I felt a pop under my hand. Lynne giggled. I stared at the rug. The pops stopped.

"Sometimes if I push a little, I feel kicks," she said. I kept my hands there until Lynne removed hers from the top of mine. I returned to my post watching the flakes in the streetlight.

I wished the imagined animal had been a lioness. Its significance would be so clear to me then. Lynne has been my lioness. She had the physical strength to work full-time throughout the pregnancy as a guidance counselor at a private high school for boys who, like their parents, weren't always eager to accept the guidance she attempted to provide. She didn't sleep well because the weight of the baby had flattened her bladder and sent her to the bathroom throughout the night.

During a prenatal appointment, I remember thinking my wife lay on the table like some maternal goddess. Her dark hair fell around her ear and onto the wax paper under her head. I stared at her neck and delicate jawline in the dim monitor glow. The afternoon sunlight shone through the sides of the blinds and fell on her hair, highlighting the lighter chestnut strands, as her face turned to look at the monitor. She swallowed down the tears that wanted to release from her eyes each time the baby moved.

The ultrasound technician squished the sensor into the blue lubricant smeared on the taut skin above Lynne's navel. The three of us looked at the screen. I know I'm supposed to root for health and not gender, but I'm hoping to spot a little dangler. I tell myself that our son needs a brother for a playmate. Bins of baby blue and rugged OshKosh are stacked in our attic. We have cars and trains and trucks. And of course, brothers are the best childhood partners for wrestling and fishing. This was what I told myself as I folded my arms and wiped the perspiration from my hands. I told myself a daughter could play sports and go fishing, too.

The nurse recorded measurements of the brain, heart, liver, and other organs. Outside, cars braked and accelerated at an intersection. A train screeched into the station. On the screen, our unborn baby's feet kicked and its body twirled to the side. Coworkers, friends, family, and even some strangers like to pretend they know what you're having. "I just have a feeling there's a baby girl in there," they might say to Lynne. "I can tell by the way you're carrying."

When people say such things, I try to force a smile, but never once have I thought, *Your logic is very convincing, and clearly you're an expert. You must be right. Let me whip out my cell so I can call my family and friends and tell them, "Hey, guess what? We're having a girl. Yep. That's right. Did we have an ultrasound? No. A woman in line at the grocery store told me. So now we don't need one."*

On the monitor we saw our baby yawn. My wife's eyes were fixed on the screen. She squeezed my hand. Her eyelashes flapped open and closed. She smiled. At that moment, I wished I had imagined a lioness in the snow, because it might have meant simply that I needed to cling to Lynne, and eventually my fears would subside.

In Nathaniel Hawthorne's story "Young Goodman Brown," before leaving for the woods one night, Goodman Brown believes he need only to cling to the skirt of his wife, Faith, to enter into salvation. Becoming a father, especially a second time, is nothing like Brown's nightmare journey into the dark forest where he thinks he encounters the devil. However, an honest man will admit that, as an expectant father, his mind is pregnant with fear.

With a girl, even though I didn't know it then, what I was beginning to encounter was the resounding feminine power within a daughter to open her father.

My wife looked from the monitor to my face. The corners of my mouth had dropped. On the monitor, I watched the white vertebrae of the baby's back and neck, and in that moment I knew it was a girl, not because I'm predisposed to psychic bullshit, but because I'm her father. There was a grace about how she moved and shifted her body in the amniotic fluid. Her position reminded me of Lynne at night, on her side amid the pillows. I watched our daughter's bones move, and she wrenched open a vulnerability in me I did not want to feel as her rhythmic heart sounds filled the small room.

As we awaited the birth of our daughter, I told myself to transform the energy of fear into the primal reaction of protecting my family. A lion defends his territory, his lioness, and their cubs. I tried to picture myself sitting beside Lynne, asleep in her hospital bed, with our daughter resting on her chest after nursing. I prepare to ask the nurses and doctors, without apology, to come back later. When we return home, at least for the first day or so, if Lynne wants to rest rather than talk and visit with loved ones, I decide to take all the phone calls. I try to take care of all of James's needs, though we know one of them is time with his mother. I wonder, though, if this idea of becoming a protective father has any self-serving purposes, since, when our daughter inevitably experiences physical and emotional pain, so will her father. If I ever discourage my daughter from playing rugby, trying out for the lead role, studying abroad in Florence, or dating a certain person, will it be an attempt to protect *her*, or myself? She will always open me.

Even in the womb our daughter could disarm me enough to wonder whether I could provide what she will need, which, of course, will change and grow as she does. And at every stage, I suppose, she will open me to see my faults, weaknesses, limitations, false presuppositions, and hopefully, on occasion, to resources of energy or knowledge or encouragement that I otherwise would have never known were there. Whether he is ready for it or not, a daughter grants a father access to the unexplored terrain of his humanity.

I traveled into unknown territory during the many disorienting months our daughter grew inside the womb. I was like a lion from another continent, displaced, trotting through thick flakes in a New England snowstorm.

I Really Need
a Fish in My Life

—⚭—

It was the way he said it that hit me. We were watching the white and orange and red koi fish surfacing, opening their large concentric mouths. They dipped back under the brown water and bumped scales before gliding away to suck algae off concrete walls. They were twenty-year-old fish, longer and wider than my forearm.

We had stepped away from the extended family, the flourishes of wait staff, and our dinners. James laid his head on the pillow of his arm, which rested on the wood railing of the bridge where we stood. Neither of us felt communicative. We watched fish as if we were watching a baseball game on TV. The movement lulled us into a stillness that hasn't been possible in the urgent commotion of our home, where the boy's newborn sister, Mary, has wailed.

He said it while watching the colors of the fish mingle in the brown pond water. He said it at first without lifting his head from the railing on the bridge.

"I really need a fish in my life."

White and orange and red surfaced and disappeared. "Daddy," he said, turning toward me, the palms of his not-yet three-year-old hands up, arms spread. "I *really* need a fish in my life." He squinted his eyes, the wrinkles in his sun-kissed face pressed for an appeal.

I didn't think about how we were standing on a little wooden bridge at the time, but I was thinking about his transitory summer—the move from crib to full bed, the combined baby/toddler class at the Little Gym he was too big for, and the piss-warm over-chlorinated pool water he choked on while trying to keep up at the Y during swim lessons. His mother and I have talked to him about using the potty, but haven't followed through. We've all been tired, and I knew that he wasn't really asking me for a fish. So I complied and punctuated my "OK, buddy" with a few pats on the head. The way my father might have done. The way fathers and sons can speak to each other when they're too tired to talk.

Building Blocks

—⁓—

On James's first day of nursery school, the teacher told us that he paced back and forth along the fence of the playground. "This is a disaster. This is a disaster," he repeated to himself. Lynne and I needed to help him adjust, but how? The teacher or her aide gave us something positive to hold onto each week, and months later, we were happy to learn that James had "married" Jane. According to the teacher, they married in the tree house on the playground, where they held hands and swayed. The boy could count on having a new friend at his new school. That day, when James came home, he built a tower of blocks. He stood before the blocks, clapped his hands, and said it was as tall as him. He's learning how to make friends, Lynne and I thought. But the following week, James sat on the living-room floor turning a block over and over in his hands. "Why doesn't she want to talk to me anymore?" he asked. The situation gave us the opportunity to give him something more important to his self-image than an answer to his question.

That summer we had replaced his diapers with underwear. We had removed him from his old day care center, and brought him home a newborn sister. We tried to hug him through these changes, and as he sat there on the floor, a hug and a few pats on the head failed to turn his spirits. I tried a pep talk.

"James, you're a handsome guy. And smart. You know the alphabet. And you can count to like . . . How high can you count?" I asked.

"Like, sixteen," he said.

"And are you fast?"

"I'm the fastest!" James said.

"So, she'll come around. If not, there's plenty of other girls in your class to be friends with," I said. But James didn't want a pep talk.

"Dad, how come she won't talk to me?" he asked again. What I heard him really asking was: How could someone not like me? How do I deal with rejection?

Lynne and I tried to recreate social scenarios in the classroom for James. We gave him lines such as: "Hey, that toy looks like fun. Can I play too?" We talked about sharing. And while those strategies may have helped a bit, they didn't quell his fears. James lit up like the red lights in the hallway during a fire drill when Jane greeted him in the morning. She seemed sweet, too. Another girl in his class said she would be his friend, but only if he ran around the room pinching each person, which he did. His grandmother heard that story while she drove him in her car. I'm glad he felt comfortable enough with his grandmother to pipe up from the back seat and share the internal workings of his young heart, but why not his mom and dad? This seemed to raise the stakes in addressing his repeated question of why the girl in his class wouldn't talk to him.

We wondered aloud while eating dinner at James's grandparents' house: Did we make a mistake by pulling him from day care? Maybe he wasn't ready. "You couldn't have held him back," James's grandmother said. "He was bored at the day care. He's so articulate, too. He needed the challenge." He's a young three. His birthday was in September. Many of his classmates turned four during the academic calendar. The slight age difference matters in nursery school.

His grandfather had a more practical solution. "Hey, James," he said, "You know what to do?"

"What?" James said, perking up from his booster seat, eager to hear words from the patriarch.

"You said Jane sits at your table. Right?" Papa asked.

"Right."

"Well, start talking to the girl next to her. That'll get her attention."

How do we help James? It became an extended family quandary, as if James was in his twenties and losing the girl of his dreams.

Sometimes when I dropped him off, I'd stare for a moment from the hallway and watch him interact at his seat. "Let go," I told myself. As I turned my back and walked between the white-and-blue cinder block walls, boisterous young voices echoed, ushering me out the door. James didn't say squat when I pressed for anything about his day on the car rides home. School wiped him out. It was the wrong time to prod. He's more talkative at night. After we cleared the dishes from dinner, Lynne fed James's sister in the den, and I gave it another try.

"Hey, James, let's build a tower," I said.

"No, thanks," he responded.

"C'mon. I need your help. We'll make it as tall as you."

As we grabbed different colors and placed one on top of the other, James said, "She still won't talk to me." *All right*, I thought. *Enough! You're three. This is ridiculous. We're making another tower. We'll watch another show. Shake it off, little man.* But it wasn't ridiculous. He was having a hard time adjusting to a lot of change at school and at home.

After we finished his new tower, James stood and struck the blocks with his fist and they clattered to the hardwood floor. Before bedtime, Lynne found the blocks hidden in the lunch cooler that he doesn't use anymore. Lynne brought the mini-cooler into the living room, so we could look at his fallen tower together, so we could try to show him that he doesn't have to hide parts of himself from us, even if they've been knocked down.

In the ER

—⟋⟍—

I looked over my four year-old son's shoulders at the wounded adults gazing across the room in our direction. Perhaps they were wondering how much longer they had to wait, or about the severity of their injuries. Behind those absent stares, maybe they replayed their accidents and the ways they could have avoided them. What replayed in my mind was coming home from work and seeing a gash in my boy's head. He was mimicking the downhill skier on TV, lost his balance, and banged his head on a table. As I zipped his jacket over his pajamas he choked back sobs, accepting the news that instead of going to bed, we were going to the hospital. The receptionist said "Anna" into the microphone, another name that was not ours. My son's eyes followed the movement of white fish in the large tank by the receptionist's desk.

In the ER

"Dad, look," James said. "The fish have blood on them." As I considered my response, I saw the two drops of crimson stain on the collar of his sleeper. He kept his eyes on the fish.

"No, James," I said. "That's not blood. It's just the color of the tips of their fins."

"Oh," he said, relief spreading across his face. We stared at each other for a long moment. I spent the day teaching high-school students, the early evening teaching college freshmen, and I hadn't seen James since I waved to him in the driveway as his mother drove away and we all departed for our Thursday. The big automatic doors to the main entrance opened as two people approached the receptionist.

When James needs a haircut, his stubborn cowlick gives him a perpetual case of bedhead. When the hairs on top of his head sprout into the shape of two ears of corn, the husks half peeled, it's an indication of how busy I've been, since taking him to the barbershop is exclusively dad duty. In the morning, he runs away from me when I try to wet and comb his hair before nursery school, and the husks shake.

"Can we leave now?" James asked as he twisted his white ID bracelet on his wrist. Until I told James we had to see the doctor, he was feeling pretty good about himself. We had left the triage room where the nurse fingered his way through the husks of brown hair to the wound. Neither of us knew we had three and half more hours of waiting.

"Probably two staples," he said, as the rubber gloves snapped off his hands.

To pass the time we made up games together. We played follow the leader, which didn't last long. We played a game of stepping on tiles and not the gray grout. If you stepped on the grout we called cracks you were frozen and could only move if the other person tagged you.

We checked in with the receptionist to see how many people were in front of us. James sat himself in the chair, placed his elbow on her desk, rested his head in his hand, and told the woman about his siblings Mary, and newborn sister, Clare. A man wheeled an intoxicated woman to the desk. She demanded pain medication for her ankle. She waved her pointed finger at the receptionist and shouted.

James and I retreated back to the pediatric section, where we sat at a small table. The TV blared over the woman's proficient use of the f-word. In the emergency room, I wasn't cutting off his pleas to evade going to bed. I wasn't standing on the landing, pointing to the second floor, exclaiming, "Up!" I wasn't thinking about the work I still had to do after James and his sisters finally settled in their beds. I wasn't thinking about how our three month-old might fuss throughout the wee hours of the morning. My objective that evening in the ER was as singular and apparent to me as the fear in the brown eyes of the boy in the green fleece sleeper and sneakers. At home his younger sisters require more of his parents' attention, but in the ER I could devote myself entirely to him. I didn't know it then, and I hope I don't have to repeat the experience soon, but my four hours with my son in the emergency room were a gift, because it gave me the opportunity to be the kind of father I wish I could be all the time.

Eventually, around one o'clock, James slumped over my shoulder. I saw his body covering most of mine as I stood before the wall of windows, his legs dangling, his sneaker-covered feet tapping my kneecaps.

With two staples in his head, James slumped over me again, his sobs eventually steadying into more rhythmic breaths as drizzle fell on the slick blacktop shining in the glare of parking lot lights. In the rearview mirror I watched my boy bring his knees toward his chest, and place his hands between them. The motor started. The interior car lights glowed orange. With his eyes closed, the corn husks of his hair rustled as he turned his head to the side. As I drove I thought about carrying him to bed, and wondered when we'd be able to go get him a haircut.

He Wears My Father's Uniform

—m—

I'm quite sure Al is the last remaining barber in town, and the only one who will remind me of my father. What I like about Al is that he's a true craftsman of a lost art. I trust him to hold shears and humming clippers to my head—to shave the back of my neck with a straight razor.

What I love about Al's barbershop is that every five or six weeks, I sit in his chair, watch the traffic on the main road in town, and he takes care of me. Nothing changes in the barbershop except the magazines and newspapers. You can talk with the other customers while you wait, if you want. But the guys at the barbershop don't really say much to each other except to defer with a head nod when Al asks who's next.

He Wears My Father's Uniform

Al's hair is white around the sides. The overhead light reflects on the skin of his head. Strands wave as he moves. If my father were alive, he would be seventy-one, which is how old I surmise Al to be. He has three children, and his daughter was born in the same month and year as me. Photographs of his grandchildren decorate the borders of his mirror. I see their faces as I see myself and Al in the reflection. I sit in his barber chair and we talk about taking care of our lawns and how we detest grubs and crabgrass. We talk about the weather and baseball.

Sometimes you have to wait for Al. You might be lucky and find him reading in his barber chair. But most times, you have one and sometimes two guys in front of you, or perhaps a pair of boys. If it's going to be a while, Al will ask if you have any errands you can do and to come back in an hour or so. You can't be impatient with Al. He's too nice, and he's too rare of a barber. It seems like an odd admission to say that I worry about my barber, but I do.

I've been to the haircut chains and other places where a barber pole spins outside the entrance. But a good barbershop should be less like a restaurant trying to turn tables over and more like Al's. For years I had tried different places before finally finding Al's place, Colonial Haircutters. Most people used one pair of clippers, and one pair of scissors. They'd ask me what number attachment I wanted on the clippers, as if I were ordering a meal at a fast-food joint. The lower the number the closer the cut. I'm pretty sure Al uses a three, but I don't know because Al doesn't have to ask. The other barbers buzzed around my head and attempted to blend the side to the top with a higher-number clipper attachment and one pair of scissors. I left one forgettable place after another in pursuit of a dependable haircut. When I think about the different faces of those who have cut my hair, one stands out on the stage of my memory. Mostly because, well, she sang to me.

Don't think singing barbershop quartet in matching pin-stripes. Think lonely woman desperately wanting someone to tell her she should try out for *American Idol*. I forget the song she sang, but something moved her to hum along with the tune over the radio, then she caught on to the chorus, which gave her the courage to mumble through the lyrics, remove the comb from my hair and hold it to her mouth as she stared into my eyes and belted out the chorus with the deep yearnings of her soul. She had short dark hair and light pink-framed glasses. She closed her eyes as she opened her mouth, which was the color of raw roast beef. I would have left, but she had yet to blend the top to the sides of my head.

Al lives in the next town over. He likes to garden. He sees his grandchildren often. And his father died of a heart attack when he was young. Al will occasionally ask me when I plan on visiting my family in New Jersey.

"Are you going to visit your parents for Christmas, or stay up here in Connecticut?" Al asks as his hairy arms circle my head. He holds my wet hair between two fingers and snips with shears.

"We'll go down for a few days to see my mom and sister and the extended family."

"And your dad, is he . . ."

"He passed away."

"I'm sorry. Was he young?" Al asks.

"He was sixty."

"Mine was too. Heart attack?"

"Yeah," I say.

"Mine too."

"Are you on a statin?" I ask.

"Sure am."

"Yeah, my doc wants me to bump up the dose from twenty to forty milligrams."

"Oh, buddy boy, I would listen to the doc," Al says, looking at the side of my head over his glasses. His voice is low, and a hint of excess phlegm rolls in the back of his throat. He shakes his head. "That's serious stuff, my friend," Al says.

"I know."

I see Al more than some of my friends, more than my mother. Every five or six weeks, James and I need a haircut, and we're not on the same schedule. After I hand Al some cash, I say, "See you in a few weeks." He charges twenty-one dollars. I used to hand him a twenty and a five and walk away. But ever since he's been cutting James's hair, I've given him thirty dollars. Sometimes I don't have exact change, and Al will take both twenties and put them in his pocket, and I have to ask for a ten back. And I tell him I wish I could just throw around twenties, and how I'd gladly throw them at him, the way some men do in the barbershop at Christmas. He says, "You and me both, buddy." He laughs, and pats me on the back.

A LION IN THE SNOW

I bring a portable DVD player to the barbershop when James needs his haircut. Al has the temperament of a grand-father. He asks James questions about the trains or cars on the small screen. When James continues to fidget after Al and I have asked him to hold still, Al laughs off the frustration and shakes his head. "I tell you, Jamie, we're almost there with this little guy. Just a little more straightening in the back and I think that'll about do it," he says. "We gotta make sure the boss at home is happy with this job."

"Al, she's your biggest fan," I say.

"Well, let's keep it that way then," Al says as the clippers buzz.

Outside the window from Al's red barber chair, spikes of grass poke through week-old snow. Cars, buses, trucks, taxis, and SUVs stop and go at the busy intersection. After a long lull in the conversation, as he stares at my hair and I stare out the window in a daze, I'll say, "God, it feels good to sit here, Al."

He wears my father's uniform: khakis and a plaid sleeveless button-down shirt.

"Well, you've got the kids in your classroom and the kids at home, right?"

"Right, Al."

"Three kids, now?"

"Yeah, Clare is five weeks old."

"And the mother, she's doing well?"

"Yes, Al, we've been blessed," I say. "Lynne's doing OK. She's tired."

"A father needs to kick his feet up too, doesn't he?"

"You're telling me, Al."

"Well, just enjoy it. This is the best therapy you got." And he continues to snip behind my ear. And I continue to stare at the shifting vehicles, their headlights glowing in the faint light of dusk.

After Al puts away the clippers, he unbuttons the plastic draped around my neck. He pushes a paper towel under my shirt collar. He rubs warm shaving cream on my hairline, and shaves it off with a straight razor. He rubs the aftershave into my skin with his fingers. I anticipate a pat on the top of my head, as my father used to do. He grabs a large hand mirror with the handle broken off and holds it up behind my head. "How's it look?"

"Like it always does, Al. Like it always does."

On Propriety

To instill a proper set of fundamental decencies about dining—that is, if you expect your offspring to model a similar level of social conduct—you must sit at the head of the table and expel the same declarative sentences you heard your own father say. Sit up straight. No elbows on the table. Chew with your mouth closed. No singing at the table. Wait until everyone is seated before holding your utensils. Wait until everyone is finished before leaving the table. Ask to be excused. No, not *can I*, but, *may I please be excused?* Try it again, the entire sentence, please.

Do not sit on a throne of inconstancy. Children sense weakness. They sense parental fatigue. Your children will suffer for diminished expectations. No matter the weariness or the tension in your neck, the tension that will claw over your skull before sinking into your eyebrows. If said claws begin sinking into your skull, inform your wife that you are retreating until the Imitrex can restore your tolerance of sound and light.

Since you are migraine-free tonight, accept the plate of steak, broccoli, and sweet potato. Remember, you and your wife decided to take shifts eating. It's hot now, so eat. Insist that the eldest child eats with you.

"Hmmm, steak," he says.

"Have a seat, please, James," you say.

"I'm not James," he says with clenched teeth. "I'm J. rex!"

"J. rex, please have a seat."

You see, children want to see if you really mean what you say. To be fair, you must accept that their sense of etiquette, like everything else, is still developing—all the more reason a father must hold steadfastly to the propriety he desires for his family.

"I'm a carnivore," J. rex says, "Roowwwl."

"J. rex, no growling at the table, please."

You lift Mary to her booster seat and snap the tray in place. Your wife places Mary's steak and broccoli on the table and asks you to cut it for her before walking back to the kitchen with Clare on her hip.

"Mom!" J. rex shouts, as he leaps from his seat to follow her into the kitchen.

"James, please sit down," you say.

"I don't want it," Mary says as you place pieces of steak on her tray. "I don't want it, Daddy." After all, you must believe that distinctive matters of graciousness must be embodied and displayed through tireless patience, and that these manners will pay tenfold in the years to come. Think of patience as the attribute you need to survive the crucible of instilling essential mores you can expect to see in perpetuity.

"James, I'm glad you're in your seat, but please sit down," you say.

"I had to see what was on her tray," J. rex says.

"Daddy! I don't want it," Mary says, her hair thrashing either side of her chair.

"Ha, ha, Mary," J. rex says. "You're a Curlasaurus."

Your wife reenters the dining room, with Clare still on her hip and carrying a bowl of sweet potato she has puréed for her.

"Mary, please don't put so much in your mouth at once," your wife says.

"Do you like it, Mary?" You ask. She nods with enthusiastic wide eyes.

"And, James, I'm not reheating your steak. Eat it while it's hot," your wife says.

"But, I don't like it hot," he says.

"It's not hot, James," your wife says. "I mean before it gets cold."

"Okay, Maiasaura," he replies. "Dad, did you know maiasaura means good mother lizard?"

"Yes," you say, thinking of the stack of library books on his bureau. "Please eat."

Curlasaurus pats her tray with both hands. Pieces of broccoli fall to the floor.

"More, please, Daddy," she says.

It's all in the confidence of the offering, like a waiter announcing the specials.

"Oh, sweetheart," Maiasaura says, as she spoons orange-potato-mash from Clare's chin. "It's a strong taste, I know, honey."

J. rex pushes himself off his chair and stomps over to Curlasaurus, arms bent, and two fingers in each hand curled.

"James, please sit down," you say, thinking of the many times you've tried to persuade him to reconsider sitting in a booster seat. You told him he could decorate it with stickers and he said those seats were for babies like Mary. J. rex growls at her, and in defense she scratches his face. "James!"

"It's J. rex, Dad!"

"J. rex, will you please sit down and leave her alone," you roar with an impatience that unsettles the pack. Maiasaura continues to try to feed Clare. You know that you don't teach young children as much as you reteach them over and over again. You know if your father were alive, and could be present for such moments, he would remind you of how hyper and active you often were as a child. The room is quiet as you exhale through pursed lips for an extended duration. You think about the times you've mentioned to James how lion cubs that do not eat do not survive. But you know trying to rationalize like that with the young boy is a desperate act. And you're not talking of lions tonight anyway. In fact, a father who talks too much in the wildness of domestic tribulation will never be heard.

Clare prefers to sink both teeth into her big toe. She holds her leg with both arms and mouths her toes. Your wife turns to you and says she doesn't think Clare wants the potato. You must see these easy appeals for affirmation. All you have to do is agree, and in doing so you will acknowledge that your wife has cooked, allowed to cool, then puréed the sweet potato in the food processor for the baby to reject the orange mash back out of her mouth. It's the perfect high-arching pitch in the summer softball league of marriage. You can't fully uppercut, and for the love of God, don't overswing. You'll pop it out of play, or worse, hit a lifeless flare out to shortstop. Keep your hands back. Get the barrel of the bat on it—a nice easy swing.

"She ate some of it last time, hon," you say. "She'll get used to the taste."

"I know," your wife says, looking at the bowl in defeat.

"Mom," J. rex says, his mouth full of broccoli, "don't you know Clare is a milkasaurus? All she eats is milk."

"You're right, James," she says, through a grin. "But we're trying to introduce new foods to her too." Perhaps endurance is the seminal fabric in the tablecloth of decorum. Be patient, and the young offspring will see your lofty expectations as a challenge and will rise to meet them.

"Mary, please don't do that," you say, placing your hand over hers so she can't scatter anymore broccoli to the floor. "If you're finished, please say so," you say. "No throwing food."

"Milk, please, Daddy," Mary says. "I want some milk."

"Did we forget drinks?" you say to your wife, knowing the answer.

"Yep."

J. rex stomps out of his seat toward Maiasaura.

"James, please, I'm trying to nurse Clare," she says. Patience! Patience will save you. It's really in the parent's ability to name exactly the behavioral expectation that will yield desirable results. Be clear, that's the key.

"Mary, please." Your wife says. James stomps back to his seat.

On Propriety

"C'mon, James," you say. You take Mary out of her seat and leave to prepare your wife's plate in the kitchen.

With your wife's plate in hand, from the kitchen, you hear, "Mary, don't eat off the floor." You return to place the plate in front of your wife. Mary continues to fill her mouth with the perimeter of broccoli she finds around her chair.

"It's good, Daddy," she says. "It's good."

James rests his head in his hand, looking down at his plate and scrunching his nose. Milkasuarus sits on your wife's knee. You ask her if she wants you to hold Milkasaurus and she shakes her head.

"She's happy," your wife says, and takes her first bite.

"Mom," James says. "Can you please heat up my steak?"

"OK, James," you say. "I'll be right back."

"I'm a carnivore, Dad," he says.

J. rex growls at the plate and spears as many pieces as he can.

Clare squeals and claps, bouncing on Maiasaura's knee, her blue eyes ablaze in the light from the chandelier. Clare is most likely the last of the milkasaurs, though your wife will say she is really the first, since the nursing didn't go as well with James or Mary. Clare breastfeeds often. She still sleeps in your room. In the morning, she fusses and your wife lifts her from her crib to her chest, to keep the other dinosaurs from waking. While Clare nurses, she lies on her side, between you and your wife, and swings her arm back to tap your shoulder, or chest, or face intermittently with the backside of her little fist. She crawls now, and locks eyes with you as you hold her hands as she tries to stand, her hips hula-hooping until she steadies herself. Milkasaurus has two bottom teeth. She drools a lot and wants to mouth whatever she can find. When you hold her, her pronounced breaths warm your ear. She climbs on you when you lay on the floor, and uses your shirt to wipe her mouth. Milkasaurus sits up in Maiasaura's lap after nursing and smiles.

The white-toothed flashes of your children's grins can overpower whatever idealistic presumptions you may have had about how you'd *like* your children to act, or how you think you *should* react to them. A smile can temporarily eradicate the self-doubt that lives in the subconscious of the chaotic parenting mind. Specifically because of its impermanence, its momentary glimpse of contentment, its ability to supersede the communicative quality of any words—you had better absorb its positive energy.

"Dad," J. rex says while chewing, placing his hand on your forearm, "is this a great dinner, or what?"

In Pursuit
of Light

—〜〜—

Our youngest calls through the dark of the morning from her crib. Streetlights and house lights blink on before the chicken sizzles in the pan for dinner, before we are all home. We are approaching the winter solstice, the shortest and darkest day of the year. Maybe that's why I continue to think about this line I heard during Mass a few weeks ago: "For all of you are children of light and children of the day. We are not of the night or of darkness" (1 Thes 5:5).

Maybe that's why I've been making so many fires lately. Our pile of seasoned wood in the yard is almost gone. It's getting colder, of course, but at least in the area of New England where we live, it hasn't been *that* cold. I've been unusually preoccupied with splintering logs into kindling sticks, making sure what's left of the wood is covered before the rain and snow have a chance to moisten the bark.

The flames licking the walls of the fireplace are simply ornamental. Yes, they warm your face and hands when you crouch before them, but a working fireplace—without the functionality of a wood-burning stove—exists exclusively as ambience.

In these momentary instances, and they are only that, when each of the three children have what they need and no one is bickering over whose turn it is to climb in the cardboard box that UPS delivered earlier, the flames wave and flash across their faces as they sit on the floor beside the glowing Frasier fir, watching the screen where Mickey Mouse plays "O Little Town of Bethlehem" with his harmonica.

This Advent season, at least as I type these words, we are all OK. In fact, we are extraordinarily blessed. We have good jobs. Everyone we love is healthy. The kids like their schools. And yet you have to appreciate that, like the children getting along, this is a fragile state of being. Like a good fire whose logs need prodding and rearranging, our inner selves need attention too. We are spiritual beings whether we are attending to the burning embers inside or not.

I don't want to get all Charlie Brown on you, but "Stuff Isn't Salvation," as Anna Quindlin wrote not long after a Walmart employee was trampled to death by stampeding shoppers on Black Friday in 2008.

Turn on any smartphone, laptop, tablet, or television right now, and eventually you will read or hear two great lies. One: You need more stuff. And two: You should be happy (and if you're not, just buy more stuff).

I've been thinking about getting more trains for my second-grader, but for now he seems content playing with the ones my father gave me. My dad hasn't been alive for fourteen Christmases. I miss him. But with a loving bride and three kids, Christmas now occasions more celebration than grief.

Earlier in class today, my students let me in on the ways their interior lives are influenced by the screens they touch and tap. We were discussing the essay "How Boys Become Men" by Jon Katz, which appeared in *Glamour* twenty-one years ago. One anecdote from Katz's essay in particular prompted the seventeen- and eighteen year-old boys to talk. The narrator came home with a black eye one day while in fifth grade. His parents called the parents of the boy who gave young Katz the black eye, which only instigated further abuse from the kids at school, who called him "the rat" for telling his parents what happened.

The students said that though there is probably less fighting in schools compared to when their fathers were young, the violence persists online, often anonymously, mostly through fake Twitter and Facebook accounts. I asked them how often this happens.

"It happens a lot," one student said, while the others nodded. "It happens a lot, but it's nowhere near as bad as it was in middle school."

"Yeah. I feel like you'd rather have the black eye because even though it hurts, it goes away," another student said. "That other stuff online never goes away. And plus, if our dads came home with a black eye, everyone would know something happened in school, but if someone is getting bullied online, the kid comes home and the parents won't know."

That night my second-grader crouched next to me as I turned a log over in the fire. "How was school today, bud?" I asked.

"It was good," he said with a shrug. "Dad, why is part of the flame blue?" I thought about how much of fathering depends on interpreting a shrug, grateful that the light drew him next to me, that his face warmed with curiosity rather than concern, that only the coals below the logs needed prodding.

The Return of
the Prodigal Father

—⊶ℳ⊷—

The two Jesuit priests in campus ministry at the high school where I teach asked me to give a talk at the father-son retreat. I watched my kindergartner buckle himself into his car seat the following morning and wondered what I might say to fathers whose sons drive. When I began teaching I was closer in age to the students than to their parents. But now, as I'm closer to forty than I am to thirty, I certainly have an appreciation for what it must be like to parent a son who strides in and out of the house with his own set of car keys.

The morning of the retreat, the fathers and sons sat in a circle, taking turns introducing the other person. The ceiling fans played with the air from the opened windows of the small chapel. Beyond the stained glass windows, cars hummed past us intermittently. As the first father spoke he shifted in his seat to lift his foot from the burgundy rug and rest it on his leg. I listened to them take turns saying something they admired about the other. I looked at the men and the boys looking at each other and thought about their resemblances, and about the quote I had just finished reading in the retreat program. "Recently, on looking into a mirror, I was struck by how much I look like my dad," writes Henri Nouwen in *The Return of the Prodigal Son.* "Looking at my own features, I suddenly saw the man whom I had seen when I was twenty-seven years old: the man I had admired as well as criticized, loved as well as feared. Much of my energy had been invested in finding my own self in the face of this person, and many of my questions about who I was and who I was to become had been shaped by being the son of this man. As I suddenly saw this man appearing in the mirror, I was overcome with the awareness that all the differences I had been aware of during my lifetime seemed so small compared with the similarities. And with a shock, I realized that I was indeed heir, successor, the one who is admired, feared, praised, and misunderstood by others, as my dad was by me."

One boy's reaction to his father's introduction of him has remained in my mind. He peered into his lap, sitting on his hands. This is my son, the father said. He's under a lot of pressure since he's in his junior year. I'm proud of how hard he works at subjects that don't come easy to him. He doesn't ever give up. He stays at it. Of course, when we talk about school we focus on the results, the grades. I don't say it a lot, but I admire how he never quits. I admire his effort.

The son didn't raise his head until his father finished. The boy's fair-skinned face glowed like the head of a struck match, the air moving over his head in the sun rays. Well, I mean, my dad works really hard, the boy said. I mean, I like my friends here, and I wouldn't be able to go here if he didn't work so hard, he said. I wonder how universally rare it is for fathers and sons to praise one another in private, let alone in front of others.

A large print of Rembrandt's painting *The Return of the Prodigal Son*, which Nouwen titled his book after, rested on one of the chairs in the circle. I liked sitting in the fellowship of these other men—men who, like me, have been "admired, feared, praised, and misunderstood" by their children.

Months ago, I spent an entire day sequestered in my bedroom, listening to the voices of my wife and three children, while recovering from a stomach bug. James was five, and our daughters were two-and-a-half, and fifteen months. The following morning, I opened Mary's door, plucked her from her crib, and let her wrap her arms around my neck, whispering "Daddy," as she exhaled a sigh of relief. Our youngest, Clare, was already up, and toddled on her feet toward me in the hall. She squealed my name, and hugged my leg.

At the bottom of the stairs, I put the girls down and saw James. I intended to rub his head—ask him how his day was in kindergarten. It was his turn to be a class leader. Instead of telling me anything, he punched me in the gut. I had yet to rub the sleep from my eyes, and I didn't see the expression on his face or his fist pulling back again. He caught me with his second jab in the ribs. The shots seemed innocuous enough for my wife to laugh, but the tight-fisted strikes hit me as more than playful roughhousing. When I followed him and asked why he punched me, he ran away and went back to his seat in the den—staring at the cartoon playing on the screen.

Before we left the house for the day, we made our way toward one another. We circled each another on the living room rug, a place where we often find each other and wrestle. I dropped to a knee, and he tackled me with all his might. I rolled on my back and he slammed his hand to the floor to signal the pin. As I thought about the punches my son threw that morning, I wondered if they were his way of telling me he was mad about my daylong absence, that it made him feel uneasy.

Though my daughters were only toddlers, I could see the differences in how they expressed themselves compared with their brother. Mary and Clare cried if I hurt their feelings or misinterpreted what they wanted. My son cried too of course, but the hurt feelings that smoldered under his ribs lingered longer, until they dripped from his eyes and the hot tears streaked his face. What I've known of the father's role has initially come from being my father's son, and I haven't wanted James to feel as disconnected toward me as I felt toward my father when I was a boy.

But this is the way of fathers and sons, isn't it—that even though we may have the best intentions, the most strident devotion for one another, like many great stories, our relationships are a series of connections and disconnections, of separations and homecomings, departures and returns.

I certainly have stared at the dark ceiling beating myself up for yelling at my children. My thoughts tend to shift, however, when I've asked God to forgive me and I realized that maybe it isn't God I need to ask to forgive me. Instead of continuing the self-interrogation, I've thought about how I could interact with the kids the next day. And yet, how is it that these little rascals know our triggers so well? For example, on occasion, when James's school has had half-days, he has come with me to work. Apparently, he found it terribly amusing that students addressed me as "Mr. Chesbro," because at home, when I've asked him to stay in his seat during dinner, or to pick up the small bits of crayon that fall to the floor and pose a choking hazard to his fifteen-month-old little sister, who mouthed everything, he said, "OK, Mr. Chez-ba-ro."

At age five, the kid already knew how to bust my chops. The mask my son saw me put on when teaching American literature to seventeen-year-old boys was a rather buttoned-up version of myself. At times I've slipped out of this formal mode to regain the class's attention, like the time I was reading a passage from *The Great Gatsby* and I sensed I had lost them. I exchanged a character's name for Kim Kardashian's in the middle of a sentence to see if they were awake. In a moment of desperation, I might even have asked them what they thought Kim Kardashian would have to say if she were asked her thoughts on the nature of Tom and Daisy Buchanan's marriage, or if she thought Jay Gatsby was indeed great, or if she had ever read a book.

However, the teaching persona my son witnessed was a serious one, and it's bothered me that, when I'm sipping coffee, in my pajamas, on a Saturday morning, my five-year-old called me "Mr. Chez-ba-ro," because it made me think he was calling me a tight-ass. I have not wanted my son to think of me as a tight-ass because, in my youth, that was how I looked at my father, who also taught high school students.

As a boy, living a few miles from Philadelphia, when we crossed the Delaware River I wanted my father to take me to Veterans Stadium to see the Eagles or Phillies play. Instead he brought me to the Philadelphia Art Museum for introductory lessons in how to tell your dad that his idea of fun—climbing endless white marble steps to stare at huge paintings with exploratory eyes—was as enjoyable as tolerating piano lessons from our next-door neighbor, Mrs. Melhorn.

When I lived in another state and turned twenty-four my father and I became friends. We were both single men who taught teenagers. We talked more than we ever had before. I was even moved to write him an apology letter for roaring at him during my parents' divorce, and for the long silences between us after I slammed the door on him, after the broken pieces of old plaster settled in the fragile walls that separated us. He died one month after receiving the letter. When I removed his belongings from the house he rented, I found the letter in its opened envelope, next to his tube socks in the top drawer of his dresser.

Perhaps one of the reasons the biblical story, "The Parable of the Lost Son," is so inclusive is the number of entry points that exist for the reader. Most sermons I've heard on this parable tend to focus on the sons, particularly the youngest, the one who asked for and received his share of his father's estate and "left for a distant country where he squandered his money on a life of debauchery." Maybe like him, we seek forgiveness. We want to repent and return, feeling at a great distance to one of our parents. Or, other times, perhaps we find ourselves relating more to the obedient older son, who "retorted" his father's request to join the celebration and said, "All these years I have slaved for you and never once disobeyed any orders of yours, yet you never offered me so much as a kid for me to celebrate with my friends. But, for this son of yours, when he comes back after swallowing up your property—he and his loose women—you kill the calf we had been fattening." Maybe that pinch of jealousy resonates when thinking about the freedom the younger brother had to adventure beyond the confines of his father's land. We can't skip over the brothers. All sons are heirs and successors to the way they are fathered, and becoming a father doesn't replace one's sonhood. But I want to focus on the father, because it continues to surprise me that that is the character I find myself relating to the most.

Upon the return of the youngest son, when "he was still a long way off, his father saw him and was moved with pity." This suggests the father was moved *from* a certain state or condition other than pity. Think about it. Isn't it possible the father was sorry too? Consider all the interactions he might have replayed in his mind while his lost son was away. Did the father wonder if his love was overbearing? Maybe the father's success seemed so large that the son feared he'd never be able to step free of his father's shadow unless he left. If one source of anger is pain, then imagine the fury that raged in the father. Because before the "father saw him," before the father proclaims to the elder brother that the younger brother "was dead and has come to life; he was lost and is found," he was simply a "lost" son—one who was "dead." I keep thinking about this interior movement, because I want to learn everything this moment has to teach me. The father "was moved" away from an emotional state other than pity, which compelled him to physically act: "He ran to the boy, clasped him in his arms and kissed him."

I wonder if we shouldn't think of the father as a prodigal figure as well. After all, it's the father who returns to the threshold of his vocation. The purest state of unconditional love that I have experienced for anyone occurred in the moments I first heard my newborn children cry, when I felt the weight of them in my arms and heard the air entering and leaving the gaps between their lips. This is a father's inauguration not just into his love for his child, but into an extreme awareness of their vulnerability, of how much they will always need him. Without the prodigal father's ability to return to this purest state of fatherhood, which is what gives him the freedom to open his arms, there is no story, no reconnection. Both men experience internal movements that propel their outward actions. When the lost son returns, the father returns as well.

The penultimate activity for the fathers and sons before they returned to the small chapel for a group discussion was to walk the campus together and share a story that the other didn't already know. When they returned, they rested in the chairs and continued speaking to one another. Father Paul, one of the two retreat leaders, asked if anyone would volunteer to go first. It didn't take long before one father lifted his arm. This was such a great day, he said. We never really get a chance to talk to one another. When I'm driving him places we catch up, but not like this. I think the big takeaway for us is just to try to make this happen more, otherwise it won't. We're both so busy.

Yeah, I agree, another dad said. I drive my son to his bus stop. He hops on, the bus drives off, and that's it. I've only been to the school a few times, so his whole day is a mystery to me. He showed me around, where his classes are, his locker and everything, and now I can picture where he is. I feel like I have an idea of where he goes off to each morning rather than him disappearing into some mirage.

I imagined this man sitting in his car watching his son board the bus and become part of the moving heads and arms in the windows. And soon, of course, the exhaust plumes, the heads bounce and bodies sway with that first jerk of the bus as it begins to lurch forward, the sediment and dirt clouding the air, the father squinting in the glare before turning to drive the other way.

James liked to jump on me when I was on the couch or in the La-Z-Boy, but I trained him to at least warn me by calling out, "Incoming." Maybe it was my father's death, or teaching high school boys, or the combination, but I was hyperaware of the temporary nature of my son's five-year-oldness. So I encouraged the interaction, the contact. Anyway, often when we were playing together he punched me out of affection, usually after he told a joke and we were both laughing.

"What was that for?" I said.

"What?" James responded. "That's guy stuff, Dad."

When James was really mad though, when he was in trouble, he said the things that children say while having a tantrum, and with words he swung with all his might. More times than I'd like to admit, I yelled and pointed to his room. What I wished I did more often was take a knee so I wasn't towering over him. Or, put my hands in my pockets and let him finish.

Upon returning from his room or sitting on the step, he liked to act as if nothing happened. I went with it, usually. He didn't always need a lecture. But unfortunately, if he was really worked up, in those instances, as I heard him stomping upstairs, downstairs, I could be found repeatedly exhaling the foul breath of regret. In those cases, when he returned, I didn't laugh at the joke he said. I told him I was sorry for yelling. I told him I was sorry for losing my patience—I shouldn't have acted that way. After the prodigal father saw his son, and after "he was moved with pity," he did not stand on high with his arms crossed and his righteous chin pointed toward heaven. He "ran to the boy." And so when James was five, naturally I wasn't concerned that he acted out. Fatherhood is not about teaching kids to be perfect, or maintaining continuous harmony with your children. Of course they will mess up, and so will we. Like the father in the parable who "clasped" his son "in his arms and kissed him" before his son spoke an apologetic word, I want to be a father who can take a punch. I want my son and me to know the pathways back to one another. No matter his decisions, at any age, I want my boy to know his father will always allow himself to be moved by the sight of his son.

Refuges and Other Forms of Repose

—◦〰◦—

Repeating the song felt like a way for a boy on the verge of adolescence to express himself to his parents on the verge of divorce. As a kid, I always heard the second and fourth lines of the chorus in U2's "Pride (In the Name of Love)" as "Want more in the name of love," but it's actually "What," not "Want." I heard an ache in the song that throbbed from my speakers and became a force field that held me in place, on the rug, as I stared at the cracks in the plaster ceiling of our Victorian home.

I sensed my parents' unhappiness and I wanted more for them, for our family. I suppose one reason I rewound the tape to listen to "Pride" repeatedly was because the song takes off from the beginning and its intense emotion reflected the dormant regions of myself where desire lived.

I misheard one word of the lyrics, but I don't think I misunderstood the tenor of emotion, the longing for "more," in Bono's voice, and in this way the song became a refuge, a place where I could rest and retreat in hope.

I remember anticipating the end of the song, pressing stop, and the momentary squeal before the cassette tape began rewinding. I'd have to guess how long to rewind, of course, and get it wrong, and then rewind more or fast-forward a little, until I could hit play again.

After I bought tickets for my wife and me to see the band during *The Joshua Tree* tour, celebrating the thirtieth anniversary of that album's release, I made a playlist of the songs I anticipated hearing at the concert. Of all the early U2 songs I still enjoy, I found myself listening to "Pride" more than any other, until I gave into its spell, and listened on repeat.

"Pride" was the band's first Top 40 hit in the United States, and was originally released on *The Unforgettable Fire* album in 1984. I was listening to the live version on *Rattle and Hum*, though, released in 1988. The one where Bono says, "For the Reverend Martin Luther King, sing," before the last chorus. As a preteen boy I knew Dr. King as the author of the "I Have a Dream" speech, a man murdered for wanting more from and for his country. In the throes of middle school, surviving personal betrayals was also a necessity.

I remember staring at the image on the tape cover of Bono holding a spotlight on the guitar player, the Edge, and listening to the crowd engaging in a call-and-response to the four beats of "oh, oh, oh, oh." The magnitude of this crowd amplified through the speakers made me feel connected to other people, to my humanity, which is what the best art does.

Details about when and where I was when I first heard "Pride," what made me want to buy the *Rattle and Hum* tape, if I ever watched the music video on MTV, or my awareness level of U2's fame—all of that eludes me now.

I can tell you that, at the concert, a family of four danced in the row in front of us, arms around each other, shouting out the lyrics and high-fiving each other after songs. And I can tell you how much I wanted to be free of paternal concerns, lost amid the 55,000 with my wife. So much of our marital life has gone into loving our three children while both of us worked. Somehow we've found ways to hold onto each other when we're both awake and our children are not.

I can tell you that on June 28, 2017, at Metlife Stadium, my wife and I stood in section 133, row 31, seats 10 and 11. When U2 sang "Pride," they displayed Dr. King's speech behind the band in large white letters on the black background of a wall the length of the entire stage. Individual words began floating from the speech. In the picture I snapped, the words *equal, truth, build, wake up, sing,* and *promise* are adrift on the left side of the black background. My wife and I sang back at Bono throughout the night. I can tell you we were there, among those swaying and singing thousands, held in place by the force field of enormous speakers.

Before the Noise
of Dawn

—ᗰ—

Every morning I try to rise before our three young children so I can drink coffee by myself in the dark. I fell out of this practice over the holidays, opting instead for the warmth under the comforter while the wind rattled the frosted windowpanes. But when we returned to our morning routine in the new year and our eight-year-old protested dressing for school, our five-year-old could not believe it was no longer the weekend, and our four-year-old turned her nose up at the breakfast foods we had in the house, I didn't have any patience for them. I was a grouch.

Waking before the children seems counterintuitive to the notion that more sleep is better for me than caffeine and silence, but it's not. Getting up before the children gives me the opportunity to orient myself before the chaotic morning push out the door. Drinking coffee in the quiet helps me to set my daily agenda, to think about the day ahead before it's no longer mine to determine.

After returning to my morning ritual, I began recalling its origin. When our middle daughter, Mary, was seven months old, I woke when she did and gave her a bottle, which she cried for immediately upon waking. We were weaning her off feeding during the night. One morning I was so surprised to wake before her, I made the choice to rise.

The noise of dawn had yet to begin. I tiptoed downstairs, and winced at the coffee maker rumbling against the counter. As the second child, Mary was born into the action of family. If noise roused her from sleep she thought she was missing a party and howled.

In the living room, I sat on the couch and held black coffee up to my face in the dark. My eyes adjusted to the glow of the streetlight creeping through the bay window. Moisture drifted up my nose and relaxed my sinuses. And my father rose out of memory with the steam. I could hear his voice boast, "Best part of the day." I suppose that doesn't place a lot of hope in the remaining hours, but I know what he means now—a sleeping house is quiet.

As a child, lying in my bed, I'd hear him bang the plastic filter holder against the counter. Water climbed through pipes to splash on itself in the sink. He woke so early he didn't fear company.

My mornings alone give me time to wonder though, as he waited for the black liquid to drip into the pot: What brewed in his mind? Did he ever consider that time prayerful, or did he simply make to-do lists in his head? I ask because the morning I rose before Mary, I felt the confluence of my roles, the conflation of being both his son and my children's father. I imagined my late father seated across from me at a diner. After he moved out, when I was in high school, we often spent time together by going out to eat. We read menus. We pulled one corner of our mouths up to acknowledge that we knew the other was tired, as if to say, "It's nice not having to talk, isn't it?" If I didn't get up before Mary I wouldn't have been thinking about how much I have missed being my father's son, how much I have wanted to be in his presence once again and sense without having to explain it that he understands my exhaustion.

I remember how Mary's cry ripped through the stillness that morning. She cried until she felt the nipple on her lips. She sucked with her eyes closed as we rocked in the chair. Her head was warm and smelled like baby shampoo and the coffee on my breath. I didn't throw my head back and close my eyes lamenting lost sleep. I wasn't trying to assess what the day ahead would be like. She sighed as she gulped, inhaled and exhaled through her nose. Because I had awakened before Mary and come to a greater awareness of my own human desires, I was more attuned to hers. I told her what sons and daughters want to hear from their parents. Her diaphragm expanded and released against my chest and forearm. "I'm here, Mary," I said. "I'm here."

I don't always think about my own dad or have epiphanies in the morning when I'm up before the children. But when they do eventually stir from their beds, I'm already awake. When they step slowly down the stairs, their small palms sliding along the railing, I'm more ready to be their father.

Notes

Epigraphs

Cooper, Bernard. *The Bill from My Father: A Memoir*. New York: Simon & Schuster, 2006. Print.

Sanders, Scott Russell. *Secrets of the Universe: Scenes from the Journey Home*. Boston: Beacon Press, 1991. Print.

Sometimes We Pray Together

Didion, Joan. *Slouching Towards Bethlehem*. New York: FSG Classics, 2008. Print.

Doyle, Brian. "Joyas Voladoras." *The American Scholar*, June 12, 2012. https://theamericanscholar.org/joyas-volardores/#

Overtime

Cataldi, Angelo. "Eagles Work Overtime For 23-17 Win 99-Yard Pass Tops Falcons." *Philadelphia Inquirer*, Nov. 11, 1985. http://www.philly.com/philly/archives

——. "Eagles Make Winning Pass Play Look Like a Marvel of Simplicity." *Philadelphia Inquirer*, Nov. 12, 1985. http://www.philly.com/philly/archives

https://www.pro-football-reference.com.

Didinger, Ray. "Jaws to Quick: The NFL's Longest Pass Play." Nov. 10, 2016. The official site of the Philadelphia Eagles. https://www.philadelphiaeagles.com/news/jaws-to-quick-the -nfl-s-longest-pass-play-18056945

NOTES

Injury Report

Hayes, Marcus. "Tra Thomas, Simon Take It Easy." *Philadelphia Daily News*, Aug. 16, 2001. http://www.philly.com/philly/archives

Sheridan, Phil. "Simon Returns to Practice After Injury." *Philadelphia Inquirer*, Aug. 16, 2001. http://www.philly.com/philly/archives

———. "Eagles End Camp But Practice On." *Philadelphia Inquirer*, Aug. 17, 2001. http://www.philly.com/philly/archives

https://www.pro-football-reference.com/teams/phi/2000.htm

Shore Break

Casey, Susan, *The Wave: In Pursuit of the Rogues, Freaks, and Giants of the Ocean*. New York: Doubleday, 2010. Print.

Zirker, J. B., *The Science of Ocean Waves: Ripples, Tsunamis, and Stormy Seas*. Baltimore: Johns Hopkins University Press, 2013. Print.

Rip Van Father

Irving, Washington, "Rip Van Winkle," *The Norton Anthology of American Literature 7th edition*, ed. Nina Baym. New York: W. W. Norton & Company, Inc., 2008. Print.

The Return of the Prodigal Father

Nouwen, Henri J. M., *The Return of the Prodigal Son*. New York: Doubleday, 1994. Print.

All biblical quotations are from the New Revised Standard Version.

Acknowledgements

Earlier versions of these essays first appeared in the following literary journals, magazines, and newspapers:

"Preface" appeared as "Inescapable Booming: On Arrivals and Invitations" in *Essay Daily*, August 2016.

"Green Mazes" appeared in *The Collagist*, March 2016.

"Trains" appeared in *Zone 3*; spring 2017.

"Footsteps" appeared as "Run" in *The Good Men Project*; March 2013.

"Overtime" appeared in *Stymie Magazine*; November 2013.

"Night Running" appeared in *Connecticut Review*; spring 2011.

"In the Paper Route of My Mind" appeared as "Brake Lights" in *River Teeth* online; August 2016.

"From the Rust and Sawdust" appeared in *Superstition Review*; fall 2013.

"I Really Need a Fish in My Life" appeared in *Weston Magazine*, issue 43, and in *The Huffington Post*; May 2014.

"Building Blocks" appeared as "What Our Three-Year-Old's Broken Heart Taught Us About Parenting Him" in *The Huffington Post*; August 2011.

ACKNOWLEDGMENTS

"In the ER" appeared in *Brain, Child Magazine*, February 2016.

"He Wears My Father's Uniform" appeared as "The Endangered Barber" in *Weston Magazine*, issue 48.

"On Propriety" appeared in *Under the Gum Tree*, April 2016.

"In Pursuit of Light" appeared in *The Huffington Post*, December 2014.

"The Return of the Prodigal Father" appeared in *Spiritus*, fall 2014.

"Before the Noise of Dawn" appeared as "Why I Wake Before the Children" in *The Washington Post*, February 2016.

I'm grateful to the editors of these publications: Ander Monson, Will Slattery, Matthew Olzmann, Amy Wright, Justin Cascio, Kari Nguyen, Mary Collins, Michelle Webster-Hein, Sarah M. Wells, Patricia C. Murphy, Debbie Silver, Marcelle Soviero, Robin Martin, Janna Marlies Maron, Douglas E. Christie, and Amy Joyce.

Thanks to the writers and editors who supported my work along the journey of writing this book: Rachel Basch, Elizabeth Hilts, Adele Annesi, Rebecca Dimyan, Andrew M. Davenport, Valerie Leff, Ned Stuckey-French, Marsha McGregor, B. J. Hollars, Anne Greene, Lucas Mann, Sophronia Scott, Steven Church, Jerald Walker, Glenn Stout, and Robert Atwan.

Warm thanks to founding director, Michael C. White, and everyone on Enders Island, the home of Fairfield University's low-residency MFA program, particularly my mentors: Da Chen, Kim Dana Kupperman, Joan Connor, Paul Lisicky, Bill Patrick, Joan Wickersham, and Baron Wormser. To Ioanna

ACKNOWLEDGMENTS

Opidee, Chris Belden, and Brian Hoover, for being the best readers and companions a writer could hope to have. Your friendship sustains me.

Thank you Fr. Jim Bowler, SJ, and Fr. Gerry Blaszczak, SJ, the former and current directors of the Center of Ignatian Spirituality at Fairfield University, for helping me see the places where light shines on desire.

To my editors at Woodhall Press: David Legere, Colin Hosten, and Christopher Madden, thank you for championing this author with enthusiasm and vision.

Lynne, James, Mary, and Clare, you were always my dream, even before I knew the way home.

ABOUT THE AUTHOR

James M. Chesbro's work has appeared in *The Writer's Chronicle*, *America*, *The Washington Post*, *Brain*, *Child Magazine*, *Essay Daily*, and *The Huffington Post*. Essays from *A Lion in the Snow* were chosen as notable selections in *The Best American Essays* series 2012, 2014, 2015, 2017, and 2018, as well as *The Best American Sports Writing 2014*. He teaches at Fairfield College Preparatory School.

woodhall press

Also available by Woodhall Press

Mentoring Teenage Heroes:
The Hero's Journey of Adolescence
by Matthew P. Winkler

Flash Nonfiction Funny: 71 Very
Humorous, Very True, Very Short Stories,
edited by Tom Hazuka and Dinty W. Moore

Alice's Adventures in #Wonderland,
edited by Penny Farthing
and illustrated by Bats Langley

A Summer That Can Change your Life:
A History of the Educational Program
at Central Connecticut State University
by C.J. Jones and Tom Hazuka

The Astronaut's Son
by Tom Seigel

woodhall press

Woodhall Press
Norwalk, CT
WoodhallPress.com
Distributed by INGRAM